Secrets of Childbirth
Tsippy Monat

Producer & International Distributor
eBookPro Publishing
www.ebook-pro.com

Secrets of Childbirth
Tsippy Monat

Translation: Shelley Sousa

Cover design: Yael Rom

Contact: Tsippymonat11@gmail.com
ISBN 9798480868890

*This book is dedicated
in loving memory to Aliza Zilbershein.*

Secrets of Childbirth

Ancient Knowledge in a Modern World

Tsippy Monat

Contents

Acknowledgments

I would like to thank the G-dess of the universe who led me on my special path, to the angels that help me and guide me to be humble and pure hearted.

Thanks to a special angel that continued to her eternal journey, my beloved and dear friend, Aliza Zilbershein, the special midwife who accompanied me for so long. To my best friend, Efrat Shaked for the endless hours she sat with me to discuss the material.

Thanks to the Hebrew editors, Noa Bareket and Alma Cohen Vardy and the English editors, Virginia Myers and Kim Ben Porat.

I thank my children from the bottom of my heart for accepting the fact that Mom is away from home so much.

And above all, I thank the women I have met along the way, the women who trusted me to help them during the most sacred moments of their lives.

Thank you all!

Birthing Rites Old and New

Margo looks at me and says, "I was a midwife since I was a small girl. My mother would take me with her to births. No matter what time of day or in what weather. In Morocco it was common that women and girls be present at births."

The wrinkles on her face move when she speaks. "This continued on during all my life in Morocco. I would assist women in the village to give birth. I would heat water, make up the bed, light incense, and pray to God that everything would go well."

She looks up at the sky. "After I had a baby myself, I began to do things differently. When I had my firstborn, I was in my mother's house. When the contractions began, my mother measured how far apart they were. My husband went to the synagogue to pray, and my father, who could not stand to hear my screams, fled the house.

"Another midwife came, checked my dilation and said, 'My daughter, it will be soon. Breathe, breathe.' I looked at my mother and the other midwife and saw that each one was doing her job correctly. They were taking care of the birth and the unborn baby.

"I lay on the bed, about to become a mother myself any minute, but I wanted a little bit more time. I wanted someone's hand to caress and comfort me, someone to be with me and give me confidence.

It was not the pain that was so terrible, nor the baby. I just wanted to be a little girl and be taken care of for a few more minutes. To be stroked and told, 'Don't worry, I am here with you. We will go through this together.' After six hours I gave birth to a healthy boy, thank God. The first of nine." The midwife smiles at me, "and ever since that time, when I come to a woman about to have a baby I look into her eyes and say, 'My daughter, do not be afraid. I am here for you. We will pass through this together.' I stroke her brow and say, 'Take another minute to be as a child until your baby will come from within you and make you a mother.'"

She finishes her story and looks at me. "Now there are hospitals, husbands who stay with their wives during delivery, but I always think about that moment. When the woman needs a little more time, another hug and a loving caress before the baby will change her life forever.

This meeting with Margo was one of my first with a traditional midwife. While she was speaking, I thought about the birth of my own first daughter.

I remembered lying in the delivery room and hearing the cry of a wounded animal fighting for her life. Then I realized that that animal was me, screaming. There was no way I could stop it. A reflex turned my insides out and thrust my child into the world. My body functioned completely without me. A huge wave rolled through my whole being and I had neither inside nor outside. I was only an enormous force that pushed out the baby. I did not exist at all.

Then I heard her. She cried and so did I and everyone else in the room. "She's here! She's here"!

Now I was a mother, but I longed for just one more minute to be a little girl.

My journey to understand birthing as a biological, spiritual, cultural, and social rite of passage began when I became a mother. Getting used to motherhood was not easy for me. I found it all very confusing. The loneliness and exhaustion, the sense of helplessness and of suddenly having no life of my own. The weight of responsibility at all times and the feeling that I was now totally cut off from who I had been before, but not sure of who I had now become. I was now a mother, but I had no role model for this.

I was born to a mother who had escaped from the Nazis when she was six years old. Her own mother had died during the escape. When I was born, my father's mother had recently died. She had contracted swine flu during the difficult winter of 1959 in Tel Aviv, Israel. As a child, I was often told about the night she died. She was burning with fever and from her bed she could see a photograph of her grandchildren. She opened her eyes and said in Yiddish, "I can't see the children." She then closed her eyes and died.

In our tradition, if a child is born in the year of mourning for a family member, she will be given the name of the person who has died. We believe that part of the soul of the deceased will be passed on with the name to the new baby.

My parents decided to create a baby in memory of my grandmother and so, eleven months after the death of Grandma Tsippora who was named after Moses' wife in the Bible, I was born and named Tsippora.

Like many other women of the still young nation of Israel, my mother had personally experienced the generation gap created by the Holocaust. She had to learn how to be a mother by herself, with no one to guide her and no one to imitate. This generational gap also influenced *my* experience of motherhood. I often had to guess or invent my role. In the absence of an historical model, I created a tradition based on shards of information and tried to piece together a broken past.

When I was in need of advice I would invoke my dead grandmother. She was like a Goddess of Life for me. I would ask her to remind me of the ancient women's wisdom and secrets, and she would help me to awaken forgotten memories stored in my DNA. She would help me to recall knowledge that was deeply burned into my memory, passed down from generation to generation.

All my life I have wanted to deepen this connection with wise old women and have sought them out. When I began my travels throughout the world I sought out older women just to be able to get a hug from them. I felt the need to be cuddled and embraced, so that I could cry like a small child without knowing why.

But that did not satisfy me. I needed more from them. I wanted to apply their methods, to understand *how* they knew what to do; I wanted to hear the secrets that had been passed down to them for generations. I longed to have their tools for dealing with both physical and spiritual problems. I wanted to absorb their knowledge of human relationships and the way in which culture influences the individual.

Slowly but surely, my searches and studies became more and more focused on pregnancy and birth. Eventually I became a doula and began to support women and couples through their birthing experience. I felt a clear and definite 'call' to work with women, couples, and babies soon to be born.

My entrance into hospital delivery rooms came naturally to me and I felt at home in them, but from the start I understood that something was not right. I felt, saw and heard a great deal of **fear** in delivery rooms. There was a big gap between what the mothers-to-be wanted and what actually occurred. I knew that this could be different.

My searches throughout the world became more focused. I wanted to understand what personal and cultural changes occur in a woman when she becomes a mother and to a man when he becomes a father. I deepened and honed my research into the intrinsic nature of birthing. I concentrated on the hidden secrets, the mysteries, wonders and miracles. I asked to be taught so that I could become a wise grandmother to the women I work with.

To this end, I became an anthropologist. Again and again I found myself sitting with a map, listening to the sound of the names of various places. The melody leads me to my next destination. I pack a bag and go. I have traveled to many places to see and learn how births based on traditional methods take place. To see how the 'field' of birth has changed over time and how births take place today.

I compare similarities and differences between cultures. Every country and every community I enter is a 'field' for research. Each one has its own social laws and local traditions that make it unique. I can only visit each community for a few weeks, and I am always an outsider looking in. I do my best to see things from the point of view of the person who is sharing their knowledge with me. In anthropology, this is termed 'seeing through the eyes of the other.'

I come to the research field as myself – bringing my personal history, my personal preferences, my beliefs and values. The meeting between myself and the research subjects becomes a part of the research itself. I am an instrument of the research. What I experience with my own flesh and blood, what I experience deep within me, what I see with my eyes, makes up the information that I collect.

There is a paradox here that poses some questions about research of this sort. Why and how is it possible to draw conclusions about specific sociocultural behavior when what is being examined is localized, sporadic, and transient? Can the information that is filtered through my own worldview and personal experience be considered valid?

I try to remain impartial and non-judgmental, but do not always succeed. I try to be aware if and when my own worldview is influencing my conclusions. I must continually refer back to myself and check where "I" infiltrates into the phenomena I am studying.

Who is this 'I' and in what way does it observe? This requires relentless self-examination and is very self-revelatory.

Sometimes I am repulsed by things I hear or see, and if I cannot differentiate between my feelings and what the 'field is telling' me, I will botch up the 'story.' For example, in The Gambia, the woman who was my host told me that she had circumcised her daughters out of fear that if she did not, they would have poor chances of marriage. She was a professor from the Wolof tribe at the local university.. A modern, educated, very intelligent woman. I was taken aback and greatly upset by her words, but because my view is not part of the story that I wish to report, I had to set aside my personal feelings.

I must constantly examine my relationships with the people I encounter, and keep in check my own opinions about everything. This process of self-reflection is part of the research, and the need to continually check how and what I see is essential. Over and over again I find myself assessing the subject I am researching by Western standards or according to my personal beliefs or values. If I measure or judge what I see and experience with Western values (assuming that they represent an objective "right" and "wrong"), I will not be able to understand situations as they really are.

The way in which I learn is experiential. In every place that I arrive at, I live among my hosts and share their daily routine. This is called 'participant observation.' I observe what is going on and also participate in it. This involvement in their daily lives gives me the direct experience that leads into a deeper understanding of their lives. When I work in fields of crops alongside the rural women, I can feel how their bodies exert themselves and can fathom things that could not be explained in words.

At other times I am only an observer.

The transition from full participant in their daily life, ceremonies and events to mere observer is tricky and happens again and again. Sometimes I find myself in both positions simultaneously. I am looking at what is taking place from outside, but I am also participating in it. The weaving in and out of the two points of reference is very fruitful and interesting. Sometimes I enter the 'field' with a certain research subject in mind and sometimes I have no specific agenda, but the topic will arise from within the encounter itself.

Whenever possible, I use a translator to help me understand not only the language, but also to explain nuances and social codes which I could never know about otherwise. The translator or mediator can give me insight into the reasons behind behaviors or the meaning of certain actions.

I ask questions and try to uncover the belief systems and traditional practices relating to pregnancy and birth. In order to thoroughly learn about the society in which I find myself, I speak with many women, men, traditional midwives, conventional medical practitioners, and local doctors (shamans).

I keep a field diary, which is an instrument of anthropological research. I write down situations at the time they occur, including discussions and interviews. I also record my preliminary reflections and ideas about what to expect, and return to these to remind myself what happened.

This journal is essential to the final writing up of the research. When I return to my normal life I reread the journals many times.

Every reading refreshes the experience in my mind. The smells and the feelings and the events all come back to me. Looking back with the perspective of time allows me to see the events in a different light. This enhanced vision enables me to formulate ideas and principles clearly and to learn from them. I am better able to analyze personal and sociocultural behaviors and to draw more comprehensive conclusions from a distance.

All birthing women, whether from traditional or modern societies, have contractions before delivery. They strain, pain, sweat, and bleed. They secrete hormones and position their bodies in similar ways to help the baby to come into the world.

As a researcher of births I try to recognize and describe the similarities of every birth and the sociocultural and biological differences. The worldview, belief system, and individual perceptions of the mother-to-be are all expressed in a singular way during the birth. The birth experience exemplifies the characteristics typical of the culture in which it takes place.

Birth is a rite of passage – a clear-cut event, full of significance, which irrevocably changes the role of at least two of its central characters. The woman is transformed into a mother and the fetus into a baby. The community that surrounds the birth also undergoes changes, because a new member is added to it and an old member has changed her status.

A rite is a planned event with specific rules of behavior, performed alone or in a group. At its heart, a rite is charged with symbolic meanings which have been agreed upon by the group. It is a behavioral system in which the senses are activated by dance, song, or the use of ritual objects, and it often has educational content. Rites of passage exist in all societies and have been practiced since the beginning of human culture. They are used as an instrument to cope with the unknown, frightening aspects of change and loss of control which characterize situations of significant meaning.

I can better analyze birth as a ritual event when I learn about the sociocultural beliefs of the women I meet in different parts of the globe. I ask them about the customs, rituals, ceremonies, parties and social events that surround the birth. But the birth itself – the physical, fleshly and at the same time spiritual event – is the real and significant rite of passage.

All rites of passage manifest the social rules of the society. Each stage of the rite is full of symbolic meaning. Every society has its symbols, which make up the fabric of its sociocultural belief system. At the birth of a child, the balance of power between the participants and their hierarchical relationships, beliefs and ideologies, are all involved.

The rite bolsters the laws of the society and reaffirms the status of community members and their functions. For example, within a society where the accepted norm is that birth is a 'medical' event, there is a clear hierarchy that will be reinforced time and again. The medical professionals who are in charge of the birth ceremony lead the way. They have the authority to make the rules about meaning and symbols.

The birthing rite expresses and also strengthens societal norms. Everyone has and knows his or her function. Core values, feelings of connection and pride in the social system are strengthened.

In the traditional world, where people are still in connection with nature, births usually take place in a female home environment. No medical technology is involved and there is no intervention with medicines or machinery. Only natural substances are used, along with traditional methods aimed at bringing the mother and baby safely through the delivery. These offer minimal 'help' during the birth. There are natural traditional tools that can quicken the labor, and manual manipulation enables the birth to occur as it should, but these are utilized only when necessary, and not as a matter of course.

The primary assistance during natural birth is to support and encourage the mother in her labor. She is surrounded by other women who have a lot of experience and the ability to put her at ease. The core belief and symbolism at work here is faith in a natural process that does not require any interference.

The more I research traditional birthing and learn about the rite, the more I am saddened and concerned about the disappearance of this ancient wisdom as the traditional midwives die out. The wisdom of generations that has been passed down from mother to daughter and from woman to woman. The wisdom garnered from countless years of practical experience, not from academic or theoretical studies.

Today, the number of traditional births is decreasing rapidly. In some places it has become illegal for various reasons, including the belief that there is an external, professional power that knows best how babies should be delivered. This stance has some clear benefits, but also some disadvantages. It is true that the use of medical technology has decreased the mortality rate of both mothers and babies, but at the same time it has caused considerable physical and sociological damage. The rise in the number of Cesarean sections performed around the world has been enormous. In some countries it is 90% of all births. This operation can cause severe harm to a woman's health.

Births that are based solely upon modern medical knowledge do not give the birthing mother – especially a first-time mother – the emotional and spiritual support that she needs. They leave her alone to face the immense changes in her body and emotions that occur in the delivery room, which amplifies her experience of being cut off from everything familiar she has known until now. This system does not provide any of the tenderness, comfort, or emotional support which are essential to get through this period of transition without harm to her psyche.

I wish to rescue the wisdom of the traditional "grandmother." To restore the touch of the experienced and trusted hand brushing the cheek of a worried mother-to-be with a simple gesture of calm. I am not romantically naive about the past. I am interested in taking the positive aspects of the old world and combining them with aspects of our new world. I would like to shape a path for ancient and modern wisdom to walk down together hand in hand. I want to enrich our culture by learning from the past.

In Western culture there are technical and other methods that are worthy of keeping. Methods that relieve pain and solve problems and save lives. Practicing good hygiene and keeping tabs on the pregnancy must be retained, of course. Women all over the world are choosing to give birth under medical supervision in hospitals, in order to reduce as much as possible the incidence of an emergency. This choice is understandable, but in its wake much else is lost.

Women have lost faith in their own capability to have a baby. They are disconnected from their bodies and feelings, and instead of these they feel fear. Fear of encountering the unknown event of birth. Women have lost control over the birth process. They have given in to the accepted Western way and abandoned the traditional way that was better suited to them.

I would say that the traditional way, combined with the modern way, is more important to women. It is true that when there are complications, traditional practices are not enough, even though traditional tools exist that can handle most situations. For example, the use of medicinal herbs to staunch heavy bleeding or various changes of position that can ease a woman during a very long labor. But traditional medicine does not have a solution for every incident or problem that may occur, nor is it effective in extreme situations. In such situations, modern medical intervention is needed.

I believe that it is both possible and important to combine the two worlds. We can create a birth environment that is tranquil, supportive, and natural inside a modern, well-equipped delivery room. Women can be given back the belief that birth is a natural and healthy event, that a woman knows instinctively how to have a baby, and that no medical intervention is usually necessary. The technology is there only to provide back-up and reassurance.

South Dakota - She Knows

One cold stormy night, as thunder raged and rain poured down, I lay in my bed, warm and cozy, and looked at the picture in front of me. It was of a group of old women dressed in colorful clothing, looking back at me. The photograph headed an American magazine article titled, "The International Council of the Thirteen Indigenous Grandmothers."

The article stated that this was a group of wise women from all over the world. They were shamans, medicine women, tribal elders and community leaders who had banded together in order to preserve and pass on the wisdom they had inherited from their mothers. Some of these women were very skilled in the use of medicinal herbs, some knew alternative healing techniques, and some could connect with the spirit world. As they looked at me through the picture I felt that they were calling to me and I *knew* that I had to meet them.

I gathered more and more information about them. I learned that not only do they teach what they know to the next generations, they are also developing new methods of using ancient tools and holding ceremonies to heal the sicknesses of this contemporary era. I learned that they met every six months, each time in the home and community of a different grandmother. The host grandmother offers her guests all the secrets and knowledge that she has accumulated, as well as the traditional wisdom of her entire community. The Grandmothers are welcome to take part in any local ceremonies, to heal and bless the people of the community and any guests who may attend from other parts of the world.

In 2004, after years of making contacts and arrangements, I traveled to South Dakota where a meeting of the Grandmothers was about to take place. I left Israel, and after a few days of air travel and driving under low clouds through the desert, I arrived at Pine Ridge Reserve, which belongs to the Lakota Tribe. The reserve is next to a small town called Hot Springs, in Middle America. This region is traditionally regarded as sacred by the Indian tribes and is also known as The Black Hills. The sleepy town of Hot Springs is made up of one long main street and a few side streets. The single-storey houses and stores look like something from an old movie. The supermarket is gigantic and its shelves are packed with enormous packages of ice cream and snacks. Many people are plus size and seem to be sitting around waiting for something to happen.

So here I am, with the wise Grandmothers. Twenty of them are standing in a circle, dressed in traditional attire. A fire burns in the center, which will be kept burning as long as the gathering lasts. The "fire woman," a daughter of the Lakota tribe, will make sure it does not go out. She adds branches when needed and sage for purification. According to local shamanic tradition, sage allows one to see beyond the naked eye and sharpens intuition. I inhale deeply.

Around the circle of Grandmothers stand the sons of the Lakota tribe, the sons of Dakota, and surrounding them approximately 200 men and women who have come from the ends of the earth to pray and be blessed by the Grandmothers. I look up and see an eagle gliding high on the wind across the sky.

I look more closely at the spiritual elders. Twenty women dressed in their tribal finery. I recognize Grandmother Rita Pitka Blumenstein, an Alaskan from the Yup'ik Tribe (and she was married to a Jewish man). She is wearing a traditional dress with white moccasins and holds a flat round drum that she has made herself. Black curly hair frames her smiling face. Next to her, in a wheelchair, is Grandmother Agnes from Oregon. She is a large woman from the Takelma tribe with tattoos on her chin and forehead. I know that she was in charge of revitalizing the ancient Salmon ceremony in which the Inuit people welcome the salmon who are returning to their source after their long ocean voyage.

After her, stands Dona Julieta Casimoro from Mexico, a tiny Grandmother with long braids over her shoulders, dressed in an embroidered skirt and blouse. Next to her is a pale woman with sharp eyes, white hair and brown deerskin moccasins. She is a Sumi warrior from Sweden. Beside her is Aama, from Nepal, who is tanned with a tiny nose. My glance lingers on Bernadette Rebienot. She is tall and dark-skinned and wears colorful robes. Someone whispered in my ear that the president of Gabon makes no decision without first consulting her.

Grandmother Rita Holy Visitor from the Lakota Tribe takes one step forward and raises her hands to the sky. The breeze plays with her long black hair and the feathers bound into it. Her face is aged with sunspots. Her blouse and thick skirt are both embroidered. She sways gently to the rhythm of the drums.

"Today I am eighty years old," she says softly. The crowd listens. "Six months ago my son was killed in a road accident. A drunk driver hit him. I invite all of us to pray for the souls of those we have loved and who are not with us today and for the pain of all mothers in the world to be healed.

The drumbeats are my heartbeats. I am sweating. It is very hot. Intense red heat. My eyes close to the brilliant sun and clear blue sky. The crowd is hushed. The musicians are also dressed in their finest tribal garb. Feathers in their hair, hands holding drumsticks or other percussion instruments. The drumming continues softly and singing begins to join the drumbeats. The sound of the drums deepens and the chanting voices rise and become stronger. I am deeply moved by the sounds and my eyes well up with tears.

I pray to heal my pain and the pain of all the mothers and fathers of this world. I pray to overcome fear and to lift the spirits of everyone I know. I pray for my mother, long dead, and for my grandmothers. In my imagination I can see my friends and close sisters. Everyone with their 'story.' I pray for them.

The drumming has become very powerful and ancient words escape from the lips of the players. Some participants hum along with the song. We all sway to the hypnotic beat of the drums. I hear many voices and feel the pain and prayers of everyone around me.

The pioneer American anthropologist Alice Fletcher realized that when the native Indians sing they are expressing their emotions without words. For them, music is a means of communication between man and the universe. Man's feelings reach out to the gods of heaven and earth. The music I am humming along with the rest of the people arises from the depths of my heart, from my pain and my longing to be healed. This singing together is a bond between me and the people around me, and between us and the ethereal.

Grandmother Rita Holy Visitor is from the Oglala, one of the seven subtribes of the Lakota, and was born on the reservation. In the language of her tribe she is the *unsi*, the all-knowing grandmother, and she has great-great-grandchildren. Her husband died when her children were small, and as someone who had to raise children on her own, she has for many years served as a mentor to single mothers. She is one of the last remaining elders who still speaks the tribal language and practices tribal traditions. She knows the ancient recipes for cooking food and preparing medicines, and how natural substances are to be used in daily life.

The leaves of the aspen trees dance in the breeze and the wind propels the white, blue and gray clouds along, above the wide expanse of the desert. The sounds of beseeching the spirit world, mixed with thankfulness, carry into space. Prairie dogs come out of their burrows and stand on their hind legs. They emit sharp cries and one dog falls over dramatically onto her side. Another answers with a yelp and the little brown critters begin to dance together, just like us. The cries of the prairie dogs warn their pack of impending danger, food sightings and other information. I think to myself that we also sing to experience togetherness and connect with each other.

A line of people passes in front of the Grandmothers to receive blessings. When my turn comes, Grandmother Rita Pitka waves a smoking bunch of aromatic sage (Salvia officinalis) all around my body. She looks deeply into my eyes, grabs my face between her hands and kisses me on the lips. She hugs me and grins from ear to ear.

Grandmother Beatrice, who is the sister of Grandmother Rita Holy Visitor, also gives me a long hug. She has a safety pin stuck into her arm with a big feather attached to it. "This is the feather of an eagle who floated above me many a time," she explains. "It fell from his wing and so I saved it. When the Sun Dance ceremony begins, you will understand why." Her wrinkles deepen as she smiles at me.

The sun paints the sky a fiery red and the fire throws sparks into the warm night air. In the center of the fire are round volcanic stones which will soon be placed in the sweat lodge. Grandmother Beatrice sits down next to me and tells me that this sweat lodge is one of the seven traditional sacred ceremonies of the Lakota tribe. It is a healing and purification ceremony convened by the tribal elders and organized by people whom they have trained and certified. The training takes years, because this holistic ceremony is for the spirit, the soul and the man's body.

The long branches are woven into arches like a semi-dome. It is covered with buffalo skins and has created a round closed tent like a womb. The entrance is on the east, and we will crawl inside through it.

Night falls. People have gathered from the area and everything is silent. The only sound is the croaking of the frogs. In the deep darkness we crawl into the sweat lodge. Steam fills the tent. The tobacco and sage leaves that have been strewn among the red-hot stones are heating up and sending out coils of scent.

The air is full of red dots, like fireflies in a dark forest. Boundaries begin to become fuzzy. Who am I and who is she and who are the others? Sound seems to enter into me through the pores of my skin. It becomes even hotter. Steam covers everything. I cannot see and it is difficult to breathe. Sweat accumulates in each of the cells in my body, even in my eye sockets. My blood feels clotted and I am gripped by fear. For a while I cannot remember where I am. Scents fill my nostrils, my sweat mixes with those around me, all is fluid and dripping.

Bit by bit I begin to relax. I feel enveloped by warmth and darkness. I feel as if I am in a big, enclosed womb. It gets even hotter. Suffocatingly hot. I bend down and kneel on the floor. My naked skin touches my neighbor's. I have no idea who she might be. My cheek touches the damp earth. It is easier to breathe down here. My mouth fills with earth. It tastes good. I relax into the heat, into an embrace, into the dark, into the sounds of songs floating amid the steam. All this happens over and over and over.

A long time passes. I don't know how long, until finally the whispering stones relax, their lights grow dim and darkness prevails. The tent opening is ajar and a breath of air wafts inside. The glints of the fire are exchanged for the glitter of the stars. I crawl through the opening and am born into the black night. My skin is saturated with steam and heat. Everyone sits in perfect silence and darkness in the open air. We sip sweet hot tea and the moon lights up the night.

Grandmother Beatrice appears again beside me, puts a warm hand on my shoulder, and strokes my face. We are seated on a log next to the sweat lodge. She asks me why I have come here from Israel. I answer that I came to meet the Grandmothers and to learn women's wisdom from them. That I would like to hear how they lived before and how they had their babies.

She tells me, "People in the reservation lived very far from one another and there was no means of communication. If there happened to be neighbors or women relatives around they would help with the delivery, but if not, a woman would give birth by herself. My mother would help women in labor but when her own time came, there was no one to come and help her.

"I was my mother's firstborn and my birth came early. My mother felt me going down into her pelvic region and she knew what to do. She told my father to boil water and to arrange a soft, warm place inside the hut. To wash his hands very well and to warm some pieces of cloth by the fire. I was born on a cold winter's night. He did all this and I was delivered straight into both their hands.

"One day my mother was called to deliver someone's baby. When she arrived and felt the stomach, she realized there were twins. My mother cut her fingernails very short, and washed her hands in soap and hot water. The first baby came out headfirst but the second baby was lying sideways, across the stomach.

"My mother knew that she must do something. After a few contractions went by without the baby changing position, she put her hand very slowly into the womb and sang to the baby. She asked him and the spirits for guidance. From outside she pushed on the woman's stomach and with the hand inside she invited the baby to come. The baby was born pink and screaming. Both babies were placed on their mother's stomach and immediately began to nurse.

"My mother would always say that the afterbirth should be hung high in a tree, far away from the eyes of strangers, so that the baby will know to grow tall. If the eagles peck at the placenta, that is fine, that is nature."

"How did she know what to do," I ask Beatrice. She laughs and says that she asked her mother the same question. "A woman simply knows," was her answer. "Sometimes we just know what to do without knowing how we know."

"Think about it," Beatrice says to me. "For hundreds of years we lived in nature. Among the trees and rivers, the buffalo and wild horses. The days and nights surrounded us. The elders taught us what they knew and today we try to teach the young what we know. The information was passed on to us by seeing and doing. How to make things, how to survive in a storm, how to grow food, how to treat disease and how to give birth. We were involved in all these processes and that is how they were passed down to us. There were no explanations of 'why.' It was simply done in that way. That is tradition."

Modern women 'know' in a different way. We need to 'understand' everything. What is happening, why and how. We read research papers and look for physiological or spiritual explanations for the important developments in our lives. That is our way in the techno world.

It seems there are two forms of knowledge in the world. The knowing 'how' and the knowing 'why.' Grandmother Beatrice and the other elders I will meet along my way continually emphasize that "this is **how** it's done." They saw and learned from experience. No explanations were offered and they 'just know.' When someone becomes ill, the shaman or healer will offer medicine or reverse a spell or perform some other action.

All of his or her options are based on thousands of years of "field research" – of trial and error and the experiments of healers both living and gone before. There was no need to explain why a certain medicine or rite was effective.

The women learned from their mothers how to behave during deliveries, how to give birth themselves and how to help others. They trusted in the wisdom that began with their earliest ancestors and was passed down through the generations. They learned from watching their mothers, and from taking part in ceremonies, prayers and trance states which expand consciousness. This is all 'how' knowledge.

Like her mother, Beatrice knows how to heal by 'just knowing.' She has no idea why certain actions work and others do not and she is not interested in finding out. She does not look for reasons or scientific explanations on which to base her belief in a certain way of doing things. For her and all the rest of the Grandmothers, this proximity to knowledge stems from the closeness of the divine, of heavenly spirits and Mother Earth.

The relationships between 'how' knowledge and 'why' knowledge are parallel to the relations between nature and culture (in the sense of civilization) and, in a symbolic way, to the traditional understanding of 'female' and 'male.' There are two forces. One is rational, focused on actions and results. The other is focused on process, and is more emotionally based. "Women's ways" are identified with nature, intuition, and primal knowledge. Men are identified with civilization, logical thinking, and actions that are performed **on** or done **to** nature. For example, cutting down trees to build boats or houses. "Male knowledge" is based on rationale and operations that control and manipulate nature.

In the West, the male rationale dominates that of the intuitive female. 'Why' knowledge is held in higher esteem than 'how' knowledge. The female forms of knowledge have been pushed aside and have lost validity. Birthing is a very clear example of this. In the past, this process was female territory and authority was in the hands of women midwives. Women had accumulated knowledge that was not based on scientific facts, but was usually impossible to disprove. Knowledge that often could not be explained in words.

Modern delivery rooms and decisions about birthing are based on a completely different model – science. The experience gathered by women over thousands of years is considered irrelevant. Traditional midwives have been pushed out, and because they could not justify their wisdom in cognitive terms they lost the right to be recognized as knowledgeable.

It is still very hot. Beatrice and I are sitting in the dark next to the sweat lodge. A large buffalo passes us on his way to drink from the nearby river. Beatrice asks me what I felt in the sweat lodge.

"There were moments when I did not know where I began and where I ended. There were moments when I was very frightened and moments when I felt protected and cocooned."

She says that at night I will dream about it and the dream will tell me things. "Now," she says as she rises gracefully, "it is time to sleep." I join Jane, an American woman whom I have befriended, and we walk to our camp.

Tomorrow, the Sun Dance ceremony will begin. This is what we have come so far to witness. This year it will be held in honor of Grandmother Rita's birthday, and the opportunity to participate in this ritual is very precious. Usually it is only for tribal members and no outsider is allowed in. Meetings have been taking place for months now to decide on the location, focus, and prayers.

Within the quiet, dense night, Jane and I can hear the sounds of the White River flowing and the wind whispering through the pines. I change into my swimsuit and take a dip in the river. Skinny dipping is out of the question. Very strict codes of dress and behavior must be adhered to by everyone at the gathering. The dress code demands long sleeves and skirts. No animals are allowed. No passing in front of the elders is allowed and under no circumstances may one go through the eastern gate. The punishment is stoning. When the elders speak, the young must remain completely silent.

When we bathe in the warm waters of the river at dawn, we can see flags waving in the wind at the Sacred Space. The space is ready and waiting for the Sun Dance ceremony to begin. We will not wash again for the next five days.

The Sun Dance is an ancient, sacred, native dance ritual that was banned by the U.S government in 1884. Not until the late 1970s did a movement begin to restore and preserve Native American culture. Since then, the tribes meet yearly to pray for the healing of anyone in need. It may be an individual, a community, or the whole planet.

The Sun Dance is a grueling ordeal for the dancers, a physical and spiritual test. They dance for five days to the sounds of drums and song, which take them into a state of trance. In this altered state they become one with the universe and may behold visions or receive revelation.

We, the guests, gather together to drink tea and have a light breakfast in the field kitchen, a ten-minute walk from the Sacred Space. The actual participants in the ceremony will not eat or drink for the five days. At night they will enter into the sweat lodge, accompanied by us (visitors) and by the keepers of the sweat lodge. They will drink one glass of water. Fasting is only one form of the personal sacrifices made by participants in the Sun Dance. It expresses the willing contribution of the individual to suffer for the good of the community.

The Sacred Space is built according to specific instructions. First, a complete circle is drawn in the earth. This is enclosed by wooden logs embedded into the surrounding ground. Four gates face the four winds of heaven and colored ribbons enclose the whole area. In the center stands a tall tree. It has been chosen carefully and brought from the nearby forest by young men of the tribe. Colored cloths have been tied to its branches, which are considered to be 'antennae' connecting the earth to the heavens. In each of these cloths has been tied a prayer or special wish from one of the participants. The tree will raise the prayers of the people upward. It now contains their deepest yearnings, sufferings, and joys.

The ceremony begins. The Grandmothers stand in a line at the west gate, facing east. Next to them are the elders of the Ogalala tribe in their traditional attire with colored bead decorations. Their grey/black hair is long, interwoven with feathers and moving with the wind.

The dancers stand silently, holding hands around the central tree, waiting expectantly. They are men and women of all ages from many tribes, not only local. Among them are some guests from other parts of the world. In the distance we can see low hills, eucalyptus trees, and the teepees and flags of South Dakota, the Ogala tribe and the U.S. flag. Any cars are hidden behind the hills and the nearest village is an hour's drive away from here.

The Grandmothers who do not dance, sit in the shade of a lean-to. A long pipe sends out fragrant smoke as it is passed among the elders. The Grandmothers use feathers gathered from many countries to fan upwards. We supporters stand in complete silence in the shade of the arbor that surrounds the circle. The sun is already shining down without mercy, and now it all begins.

The eldest member of the tribe is Milo Holy Visitor. His black eyes look out earnestly. As he drums softly, he says, "My Grandmother and my aunts raised me. Women are the mainstay of the Lakota Tribe. You, the elder women of the tribe, are our teachers. I stand in awe of you *unsi*. Grandmothers of all the world look up to you. I honor you and bless you with the strength and wisdom necessary to lead us in faith. I humbly thank you." Hands beat softly on the stretched skins of the drums. Grandmother Rita spreads her palms to the sky and says, "We have gathered here in order to transfer ancient knowledge to the next generations; for the seven generations to come. Our aim is to save our tradition and train the young of the modern age. We wish to re-link humanity to the Earth.

"We, the Earth and the language are one. If we disregard any one of these three, we will no longer be who we say we are. After a long period of forgetting, purposely or not on purpose, we are gathered here now to remember. To remember ourselves, our ancestors and our traditions. It is up to us to take care of the children and to teach them what we know. Both the family and the tribe are of importance. That is why we must fortify them." She speaks now in her tribal language, "Ingloaya Awi Naaji Vi."

"Someone is ready. I am always ready. To stand up. In these days serenity is a rare thing. We will pray today for serenity. Our aim is to return the peaceful balance between nature and man."

Feet begin to stamp in rhythm with the drums. For many weeks the dancers have been preparing for this event. They prayed for guidance from the Heavenly Winds and looked inside themselves to determine the true purpose of this year's Sun Dance ritual. Now they are ready and will dance around the Sacred Tree for four days. The stomping of feet answers the drums. Sacred songs burst out from the throats of the dancers. From deep within they plead with Mother Earth and the Winds to heal pain and suffering. The aim is to offer personal sacrifice for their families and the community. They beg forgiveness for the destruction that man has wrought on his environment. Dust rises from the dry earth as the chants arise from the depths of their lungs.

I join in the singing. In one of the many stories the Lakota tell, the world was formed by the stamping of millions of buffalo galloping in the desert. They stamped down the hills until ravines were formed, and from these cracks the universe was created. Perhaps a new universe will arise from the dust we are creating here. The heat is smoldering and the concentration of the dancers is intense.

Some close their eyes and dance for hours on end. Clouds roll by, minutes pass, my eyes mist over. The music enters into me and I move without thinking. Sounds enter my body and flow through all my cells and the beats move me from within. My eyes close, my mouth relaxes, step, step, step, step, my body vibrates effortlessly. I see the sunlight through my eyelids; sweat accumulates and my heart beats with the drums.

I do not know the tunes, but I sing along with them in perfect sync. Sometimes a thought will enter my brain and report to me what I am feeling. It returns me to the space I occupy, and thoughts like when will this be over, when will we eat, come to me. But most of the time I do not remember who I am, where I come from and where I am. There is no division between myself and the world. I have no body and no physical boundaries. I do not feel the difference between my foot and the earth it steps upon.

The minutes and hours flow together into one smooth passage of time. The fasting, the dancing, the drums and the blazing heat all merge to create the trance. By the second day I am very aware of the stench that is coming from my unwashed body. It seems unbearable, but by the third day I no longer smell a thing. They say that by the fifth day you don't see why you ever bothered to shower at all. We shall see.

At some point during the third day, the dancing suddenly stops. In the ensuing silence a man walks into the center of the Sacred Space and stands beside the tree. Other men surround him, calling upon Mother Earth and the Ancestors. They insert a ring of well-sanded bone under the skin of his shoulder blade (scapula). I feel a sharp pain. The bone they have stuck into his back also sticks into mine.

The man stands tall, gazing into the distance. His mouth is relaxed. He is here but also somewhere else. Another ring is embedded into his other scapula. More bones are inserted and then all of them are attached to long ropes. These ropes are then thrown up and held by the top branches of the tree. The man's legs leave the ground and he is suspended by his shoulder blades between heaven and earth.

The drums become louder, but a hush seems to surround me in which I can hear my own breathing and feel Jane behind me, convulsed with pain. The crowd stands still, and I notice once again the eagle soaring in the sky above us.

Another man is embedded with bone rings to which are attached ropes tied to huge buffalo skulls. The man begins to drag these skulls around the circle to the beat of the drums. His eyes shine, his mouth is agape and his skin glistens with sweat, but not a drop of blood can be seen on his back.

A third young man is raised up to the tree top leading to heaven. His face is completely relaxed, his eyes are bright. Ropes are tied to rings and put under the skin of more strong young men. Buffalo skulls are tied to more rings and men, and they too begin to run in a monotonous rhythm, dragging the skulls and raising dust.

The drums beat softly and continuously. Low sounds are emitted by the singers. Eyes look up to the sky, to the young men who are suspended. The dust thickens, the skulls carve deep troughs into the earth. One young man comes down from the tree. He shakes himself and looks around. He is not yet really here. Jane and I hug each other.

This is not the first time I have witnessed people in states of trance or altered consciousness. It is not my first time to experience a trance state myself. There must be a period of transition between the cosmic and the concrete. I have read that during a trance, the brain function undergoes changes and now I feel this happening to me.

The trance, as I experience it, seems to creep in under my skin along with the heat, the repetitious music and my sweat. I find that my perception of time and space has changed. At one moment I can look at what is happening as an observer. I can even go along with Jane's cynicism, and become judgmental and critical, but the next moment I have entered into a state where space and time have no importance and there are no thoughts 'about' anything. My body moves itself unconsciously and I do not feel it. Strange emotions arise within me and I do not really know where I am. My perspective on day-to-day things that are usually important to me has changed, and my mind does not work in its usual fashion.

The neocortex part of the brain, which is in charge of analytical thinking, is functioning at a very low level, and most of my brain activity is now concentrated in the 'primitive' limbic system where social norms are irrelevant. My throat emits sounds that I normally would not dare to voice.

Peter Levine is a researcher of the subjective, mystical experience of trance states, and coined the phrase "felt sense" to describe a sixth sense which combines all of the five senses together as one. I can feel this now – all of my senses are integrated. It has been found that during a trance, the connections between parts of the brain deepen. Some areas of my feelings are cut off, but at the same time I experience some senses differently from usual. My sight becomes sharper, hearing is enhanced, colors are brighter and more vibrant, and I am acutely aware of all that is going on around me. I enter a world of mystery, and new insights are revealed to me. I do not always remember them afterwards, but I know that I have absorbed them into my being, and that what I learned in a trance state will be useful to me at some point in my normal life.

During the birth process women experience trance states. I have seen this many times. The birthing mother retreats into herself, in deep concentration. She is being flooded by hormones which induce her to be aware only of herself, and not of other people or her surroundings. When my own daughter gave birth she gave words to this feeling: "I am floating, I am high, I am in the zone."

When conditions allow, the birthing mother will begin to move around in the area without being aware that she is doing so. Her pupils become dilated, her skin reddens, she hums and snarls. She cannot answer questions put to her and will sometimes demand silence from the people around her. When she reaches the final stages of delivery, when the birth canal is fully dilated, just before the baby comes into the world, the birthing mother loses all sense of 'etiquette' and can be downright aggressive. She throws off all social taboos and is concerned only with herself. This is a singular form of trance caused by the endocrine system only during the time of delivery.

The renowned French obstetrician Michel Odent is one of the modern pioneers promoting natural childbirth. He speaks of the 'hormonal dance' .The womb, which is usually the size of a fist, will expand up to six times this size during pregnancy. The amount of blood in the bodies of pregnant women will also be considerably more than usual, and as a result her blood vessels widen. The ligaments that attach the womb to the pelvis become longer and those that support the pelvic joints, hip joints and rib cage also widen. This is to give the skeleton the necessary freedom of movement to accommodate the expanding womb and fetus.

When a woman enters into labor, the hormonal cocktail changes to create contractions in the womb and to widen the pelvis for the baby. At the actual birth, further hormones are secreted which contain oxytocin, endorphins and adrenalin. Their job is to assist the baby on his way from the womb into the world, to produce and release milk, and to cause bonding between mother and child. In order for this unique hormonal system to work optimally the mother must feel safe, protected and loved. The oxytocin will only release into a relaxed, environment with no disturbances.

We know this from observing mammal births. The female will look for a dark, safe place to have her babies. Her survival instincts tell her that she needs a secluded environment, a place that provides protection for her newborn and defenseless young. The scents of blood and other secretions may attract predators. If a mammal senses that she is in a dangerous situation, her body will not secrete oxytocin and the birth will not take place.

At the very hour of birth, most of a mother's brain function will take place in the limbic (survival) areas of the brain. The secretion of adrenalin during the actual labor will cause a reduction in the amount of oxytocin released.

Signs of danger deflect the brain function from the limbic area, as does any situation that makes demands of the mother and requires logical or social behavior on her part. These will cause the hormonal secretions to decrease and prevent the baby from leaving the womb. Only at the exact time that the baby emerges will the levels of adrenalin and oxytocin increase. This ensures that the mother is extremely alert at the moment her defenseless baby is thrust out into the world.

The trance state that birthing mothers enter is similar to the trance state in shamanic rites. The birth mother will also sway in a repetitive motion, and the heartbeat of the baby inside her is 140 beats per minute, the same as the drumbeats in the ceremony. Her brain secretes a mixture of hormones. Oxytocin is released into her body to cause contractions. Additional hormones are secreted when the baby's bones come into contact with the mother's pelvic bones. Opiate substances are secreted – natural pain relievers that cause very deep relaxation, while at the same time allowing the mother to be intensely alert. Brain function moves to the limbic areas related to the more primal parts of our natures.

The touch of the baby on the inside of the pelvis leads the mother to move her body unconsciously in order to ease the baby's way out. She will not be aware of space and time in the usual sense. The sounds that come from deep down in her throat help her sphincter muscles to open. The voicing of these sounds also causes her lungs to empty, giving room for fresh air to enter, which enhances her ability to cope with the huge physical effort required to push out the baby.

I find myself in a trance now, not unlike those I entered during the births of my four children. I am no longer merely an observer of the ceremony. I am here in the blazing heat, my inner beat is perfectly in time with the beating of the drums. I feel in my body what the dancers feel in theirs, I hear the same sounds, smell the same odors; I feel the hot air, the touch of cloth on my body, the shrunken stomach.

I expand endlessly with no boundaries. I understand many things without words. I am not connected to time and space. My movements to the music are automatic, without thought, and the sounds I utter flow out of me without my interference. I do not feel tired. I am completely here but also not here at all. I can watch myself as if I am dreaming about myself. I can leave my body. My energy rises up, my pains are left behind. I am part of everything and there is no separation between the universe and myself.

A traditional midwife does not know how to explain the relationship of the hormonal system to the emotional and physical experiences of a pregnant woman. They do not have the scientific evidence to hand, but 'just know' that a woman in labor is not to be disturbed. That she needs to be in a protective and warm environment and must be encouraged and supported emotionally. They require no explanations; they simply act according to what they have witnessed since the beginning of time.

When I am present at a birth where the mother enters a trance state, I clearly see her involuntary body movements, her inability to deal with medical matters, and the way that the people around her and their concerns with everyday things disturb her deep concentration. I see how these disturbances, very quickly, negatively influence her contractions and progress.

The Italian midwife Verena Schmid researched the subject of hormones during labor. According to her findings, hormones are released during the entire pregnancy. They become stronger during labor and will continue to be secreted even after the delivery, when they function to create a bonding between mother and baby and to allow the special state of awareness created at the birth to continue. The baby also absorbs these substances – especially oxytocin – and this special state creates ideal conditions for mother and baby to fall in love with each other.

Oxytocin is referred to as "the love hormone." It is secreted at times of intimacy, when couples are in sexual congress or when a person is feeling loved and safe in social situations, and reinforces this behavior. It is especially important in the bonding between mother and baby. All these are rational, scientific explanations of 'why' and explain the biological processes to us.

If we explained this in rational terms to modern medical professionals, would birthing mothers then be allowed to go into trance states during their labor? Would they be able to fully enter this state without being disturbed? Perhaps we can create conditions that will permit the natural hormones to do their work in a Western, technological delivery room.

Is it possible that some of the problems of violence and alienation in our modern world may be due, at least in part, to this failure of permitting hormonal secretions to do their job of promoting love and connection at the earliest stage of life?

During her labor in a modern delivery room a woman is faced

with many stressful situations which are not part of the natural childbirth process. In fact, the importance placed on childbirth as a pathological process *increases* stress. There are almost continual disturbances during a typical modern birth and they will force the mother to use her rational brain, which will reduce oxytocin levels. The use of epidurals and other anesthetics as routine procedure also reduces the amount of oxytocin in both mother and baby.

Dr. Odent speaks of the danger to humanity brought about by this lack of love during the critical birth experience. This may sound radical and extreme. Women will ask, "Are you suggesting that because I had an epidural I love my child less?"

This is a deep and important question that should be given careful consideration. The mechanisms of connection and communication in human beings are complicated and intricate. I believe that understanding the fact that using anesthetics during the birth will affect these mechanisms will allow people to make different choices. Just being aware of these facts will go a long way to help women decide how to create a space where even if anesthetics are used, they will not interfere with their natural hormonal system.

Entering a trance state that will encourage the secretion of beneficial hormones can be handled in a controlled manner inside the modern delivery room. Even if the birth mother has decided to use some form of pain management, such as an epidural, she can still enter into herself if she is in a relaxed, loving and trusted environment.

A birthing mother in a state of trance will continue to experience the physical pain of contractions while being flooded with opiates secreted by her own body. Her energy level is being raised and she is gaining power, along with an ecstatic feeling. By the time the baby is ready to come out, the mother has become a volcano waiting to erupt. A huge wave engulfs her and her self-control slips away.

Pressure rises steadily at the entrance to the birth canal, the anus, and the clitoris, and she must surrender completely to this force over which she has no control and which is impossible to stop. It is the reflex that moves the baby into the canal. She twists and turns, from within and without. The baby is coming, the head peeks out, the head crowns, the widest part of him causes an impossible stretching and burning at the vaginal opening. Everything is pushed aside, the clitoris is at the height of excitement and a minute later – the head is out! And immediately after this the shoulders and rest of the body slip out.

The baby is finally out! The mother is euphoric, in love, completely drained, sweaty, trembling and happy. She is smiling, laughing, crying, in love with all the world and especially with the newborn baby she has given life to. This tumultuous experience has been described as the one which surpasses all others.

Just as the trance ritual is used as an instrument to unite and deepen connections between individuals and their societies, so at birth a trance creates a strong bond between a mother and her baby. This connection will help her to fulfill the demanding role of motherhood.

If we learn the secrets of traditional midwives, how they inspire and uplift the birthing mother, as well as learning the physiological and emotional mechanics which permit the secretion of oxytocin, we will be able to progress on both of these fronts simultaneously. By combining modern and traditional knowledge we can give a pregnant woman the option to connect with her inner power.

"A woman just knows," Grandmother Beatrice told me on that first night in the sweat lodge. After the ceremony was over, I understood what she meant. They 'know' because they are familiar with the doorway they pass through and they arrive at knowledge without having to 'learn' it. Through the gateway of trance. We in the West have forgotten that a gateway even exists.

"Do you know how to give birth?" is a question I always ask the women I work with. In many cases an embarrassed look comes over their faces, or they say no, they don't know. Some answer that their bodies know but not their minds. They think that in order to know what their bodies know they must also learn in their minds, through books, lectures, etc. So they read books, sign up for pre-natal class-es and acquire theoretical knowledge, and then they feel yes, they know. Learning replaces the "knowledge that has no words."

This is fine, I am not criticizing them. In fact, I think that the use of research today about the makeup of the body and psyche allows pregnant women to feel more relaxed and better able to enter the trance state that their body is directing them into. Paradoxically, understanding the process scientifically can open the gateway to the "other" form of knowing.

The pregnant woman learns about the existence of the doorway through which she can pass to an expanded state of consciousness. If she now knows that this knowledge exists inside her, and she has the confidence, she can relax and surrender to her internal process-es, which happen intuitively. If the people around her during her pregnancy and the birth realize the importance of this process and are knowledgeable about it, they can help her to retain her medita-tive state in a relaxed environment.

When I accompany a woman during pregnancy and birth I come equipped with both forms of knowledge. At the time of the birth I join her in her internal voyage, in the same way that I joined in the trance in the intense heat of South Dakota.

On the last night, after the sweat lodge, Grandmother Beatrice and I sit together once again. She is in a chair and I am next to her on a wooden stool. I ask her why they only insert the bone rings into the men.

"Physical suffering shows how much a man is willing to go through for connection with the spirits. Women go through pain when they give birth. When we are giving birth we are directly connected to Mother Earth, to the spirits and to the ancestors. We are continuing the lifeline and so we do not have to go through the suffering again at the ceremony, but in order to identify with the men, I and other women who dance will insert a safety pin.

"This morning when I danced in the sun with the rest, I did not feel any pain or hardship. I am no longer young. I was fully concentrating and not aware of any details around me. I felt only the sun and the sounds. The drums were not coming from outside of me, my body was the voice of the drum.

"It reminded me of my birth experiences. It feels the same. Complete concentration, I did not feel that I am in some place, where, if someone tried to speak to me, I could not answer. I asked my husband to sit to the side and drum very very softly. I moved and breathed to the rhythm for hours.

"I have danced on this earth for many years, but every time is different. Sometimes I meet with people from the past and they tell me things. If someone comes to me for advice, I can close my eyes, feel the feet that connect to the ground and words begin to come out of my mouth. Wisdom comes to me from the spirits and from the earth and from the sky. It is simply so. After it happens many times, it is possible to enter into this state very quickly and 'just know.'

She places her warm hand on my shoulder and I lean my head on her knee and we are silent.

Alaska - Rite of Passage

Finally, I am walking next to Grandmother Rita Pitka Blumenstein in Anchorage, Alaska. She is an elderly Inuit from the Yupik tribe. I met her for the first time at the Gathering of the Grandmothers in South Dakota and I fell in love with her.

I have come to Alaska especially to meet with her and to take part in a ceremony that she will conduct with other community elders. I have tried many times on this trip to meet with her. I want her to teach me some secrets of healing. When I first arrived in Anchorage, I called her. She was excited to hear that I had come from Israel, and every time I happened to bump into her she seemed happy to see me. She never said no, but during my entire visit so far, I have never gotten the chance to sit alone with her. She always managed to avoid it.

But now, here we are, walking side by side. The fragrance of pine floats in the cold air and I must lengthen my stride to keep up with the 80-year-old Grandmother. I know that she still works with pregnant women, so I ask her if she still serves as a midwife. She turns to me and laughs (she's always laughing), "Work, work," she answers. "I always work, according to what needs to be done."

We are surrounded by many people, but I decide to try and make use of this opportunity to get advice from this feisty lady. "Grandmother," I say, "What do you do with the women you work with? How do you help them? Would you be willing to teach me some methods, give me some tips, some special thing you know?" I am practically begging. She stops in her tracks, grabs me by the shoulders and laughs. "How can I know? I don't know anything. Only when I meet the woman with her mate, then I know what to do. She releases me and continues her brisk walk to the big circle, where everyone is awaiting her.

This is the meeting *before* the ceremony of dancing and singing that the leaders of the North American tribes have planned. It is a meeting of the local Inuit Tribal Elders and the Council of Wise Grandmothers. In the large circle sit women of all ages and the Grandmother in her traditional clothes, smiling. I stand not far from her, see her turn to one of the younger women and ask her how are the babies of her tribe. The young woman looks slightly embarrassed and answers that she recently discovered that she is pregnant.

Grandmother Rita begins to speak. She is telling the crowd that she was raised by Grandmothers. She continues, explaining that she learned from the Grandmothers but found her own way of doing things ... and she feels connected to all the Grandmothers in the world. She is almost 80 years old and says she doesn't know anything. When she told me about her work with the pregnant women, I learnt that she was born to a shamanic family from Nelson Island. Her grandmother could 'see' things and her mother was a healer. Her grandmother taught her how to use medicinal herbs. Grandma Rita Pitaka always says that we grow up in water and we are created from water. She says that old people become dry and have to drink a lot of water. As a traditional midwife she has helped many women.

After the baby is born she used to put her finger into the amniotic fluid and touch it to the lips of the baby. She blesses him that he will always be clean.

She continues on to tell that she was born in 1939. Her mother was widowed a month before she was born. Her father was a fisherman and died. She grew up on the island with her shaman grandfather who taught her to use medicines, to look and to learn – she says this with a smile.

"The meaning of my name is 'tip of the tail that cleans the path to the light.' I see myself as one who carries the tip of the tail of the olden times into the modern times. My grandfather once gave me a bowl with spiders inside and told me that that is my life's purpose. I was very young, and did not understand what he meant. Only years later did I understand that he was referring to the web – that of the spider and that of the Internet. I am the junction at which the generations meet." (*Grandmothers Counsel the World*, by Carol Schaefer, 2006, p. 45.)

Grandmother Rita is the first certified traditional midwife in Alaska and she worked for many years in the tribal medical center. I do not know if she is trained in Western medicine, but among her community she is considered a doctor.

The Alaskan government supports the preservation of traditional wisdom and ancient shamanic practices alongside modern medicine. The government declared Grandmother Rita to be one of the leading women in the country, and any new government agency only opens after Grandmother Rita has given it her blessing. There is a special Rita Pitka Blumenstein Day in Alaska when Yup'ik heritage is celebrated. She still teaches Yup'ik culture in various frameworks to this day. She trains her granddaughters to become healers and expert herbalists.

"My mother taught me that her stomach was my first home," Grandmother Rita continues, "and whatever she did while I was inside, I learned. To be in a womb is like being under the ice. You see and hear everything, but not clearly. The light is dim and the sounds muffled. In our worldview, everything is round. There is no high or low and no one is more important that anyone else, and man is not more important than nature. Death is part of life. Death is healthy. The dead continue to act in the world in other guises. For example, as animals. Our dancing symbolizes the interdependence of man and nature in all of its varied forms and behaviors."

This summer the Holy Ceremony will be held in the park under the auspices of the city of Anchorage. In the distance the frozen Denali Mountain Range can be seen. The sky is very blue with a few white clouds, and the grass is very green. Cars drive on wide avenues around the outskirts of the park and all of us, young and old, dance the traditional dances to the beat of the drums and the sound of songs sung in the ancient tongue.

The indigenous people are all in traditional attire, which consists of short cotton skirts in shades of blue, pants of the same fabric and shin-high moccasin boots. The boots are decorated with colored beads and topped with fur. The dancers hold fans of white feathers, also decorated with fur, and wear headdresses of fur and feathers.

The drummers sit on one side. Each of them holds a drum he has made himself from a large hoop of wood. The skin is stretched tight and held in place by straps. On the drums are designs from the living world. Every drummer has his personal symbol. The songs and dances are slow and rhythmic, as are the movements of the dancers. They bow from the waist and then bend their knees. They fan upwards toward heaven.

Marie Meade is Grandmother Rita's friend. She is also a Yupik elder who believes and strives to pass on the Yupik wisdom. She teaches song and dance at the University of Anchorage. She has taken me under her wing, here in Alaska. She teaches me the dance.

I am wearing a feather headdress and am bowing and fanning along with the others. The music is monotonic and the dance repetitive. They bow, wave their hands, sway their heads, and the feathers respond to the movements. I catch the rhythm and Marie signals to me that I am doing it correctly. She has explained to me that the dance represents the animals that live in this environment. The animals in their physical bodies as well as their soul throughout its many lifetimes. My body can sense this idea of continuation, the belief that the animals are part of our ancestry.

After the ceremony, Marie Meade tells me that I should meet Palaskovia. "She is my dear friend and she can tell you about birthing in the olden days." Marie speaks with a heavy Inuit accent full of guttural sounds. "Tell her that I sent you and make sure to bring her something fresh."

"Like what?" I ask. I already know that I will go. "What should I bring?"

"Oranges," Marie says decisively.

The next day I am floating like a bird in the Alaskan sky at the end of the world. I am on my way to a little village, which can only be reached by plane or by three or four days sailing on the river. In the little plane are six other people, two mailbags and four bundles of supplies for villages. We fly over the Bering Sea to the east of Anchorage. The sun lights up the cold air and the fishing boats and oil rigs dotted across the sea. The eternally snow-covered mountain ridges spread below us are shining and brilliant white. When the winds shake our plane I think that if I were to die now, at least it would be among all of this dazzling beauty.

When we land, I look around at the flat windswept plain. I am cold and trying to transition from the shaky plane ride to the freezing air in this place. I am nervous and shivering from the cold and from fear of the unknown. Will I be welcome in this place, will I be able to communicate, will I find material for my research?

As I stand on the frozen runway with my overflowing bag of oranges, it becomes clear to me why I was asked to bring them. It is so cold here, and the ground is hard almost all year long. Only very strong plants can grow and produce anything edible. There are some bushes growing here that are covered with blue and red berries. They are round and sweet and full of vitamin C. They will be stored and kept for the even colder days of winter. Now it is summer. It gets light at 3 a.m. and the sun sets at midnight. These are the long days of sun. It does not give warmth, but at least its light shines for many hours.

I am driven in a very noisy ATV to the midwife's house. When the door opens, I enter a large vestibule. On the walls hang kitchen utensils and farm implements, various items of clothing, and bunches of drying plants. Circular rows of large shoes are arranged around the walls. I am invited to remove my shoes and am given fur-lined plastic shoes. The Yupik driver explains in a few words that shoes must be taken off to protect the house from mud and slush.

Now there is another heavy wooden door. When it opens, a waft of warm, steamy air greets my face. The man directs me to wait in the warmer area while he goes back to the vestibule to change his own shoes. In this second hallway the walls are hung with coats, snow suits, face masks, scarves, hats and gloves. Here we remove our scarves and coats.

We go through yet another door and I am inside the house. There is a kitchen, dining area, living room, shelves, closets, and pictures of Christian holy men and family members hung on the walls. Everything is size XXL. The couches are huge, the fridge is wide, the table gigantic, and a very large TV hangs on the wall. Pala Palaskovia herself is a very big woman with the characteristic flat, square face of the Inuit people. She is sitting in the middle of a couch in the middle of the room. She doesn't move, doesn't smile, doesn't say a word to me. She just looks at me very seriously.

I say "Hello." No response. I introduce myself. No response. I take out the oranges, wonder what to do and then offer them to her. "Marie sends you her regards."

She accepts the oranges from me while sitting on the sofa, but does not say a word. I stand there feeling uncomfortable. I don't know what to do with myself. Paula squeezes the oranges, grunts some unintelligible syllables and takes one out of the bag. She smells it. Then she looks at me. "Marie told you to bring them for me?" she asks gruffly.

"Yes," I answer. "I wanted to bring something you would like and I didn't know what, so she said oranges would be good."

"She knows what I like," she replies, still gruff. "How is she?"

"Very well," I answer. "She sends you her regards and asked me to tell you that all the children are well. She has a new granddaughter, one month old. There was a meeting organized by Grandmother Rita Pitka Blumenstein and it was very useful and important.

Another grunt. I don't dare to move.

The old Inuit woman bites into the orange, puncturing the skin, and begins to peel it with her large fingers and rough nails. The wonderful aroma floats into the room. She is concentrating on the orange. She peels off a piece, studies it, and then opens her mouth and chews it slowly. Bite by bite the peel disappears. The old woman now turns the peeled orange round and round, studying it with great concentration. She separates it into sections. Each section taken from the orange is placed very carefully and respectfully onto her thick skirt. Another orange segment and another. The scent mingles with the other smells of the house. Smells of cloth and wool and cooking.

I shift my weight from side to side. Long minutes pass in further contemplation of the orange. It has been transformed from a perfect orange ball to pieces of peel and has now become an artistic exhibit of segments arranged on the surface of her skirt.

Pala raises her eyes to mine. She suddenly remembers that I am here. She gestures to the sofa. Is this a signal that I should sit down? I am afraid to err and continue to stand. She mumbles something and pats the sofa. I begin to inch forward very slowly. Paula goes back to the orange Takes up one segment, sniffs it, opens her nearly toothless mouth wide and chews.

Suddenly the door springs open and a sturdy, good-looking man of about 50 makes a loud entrance. This is her son Jo. He takes off his fur coat and his layers of warm clothes, approaches me without hesitation, shakes my hand warmly and immediately begins to question me.

"How are all the friends of Marie and Rita in Anchorage? How was your journey? How is the weather there? What clouds were in the sky in the past few days? Did it rain and did you see the village yet?"

While he is asking, he also fixes me a cup of hot tea and asks if I had eaten yet and says how nice of me to bring oranges. His square face lights up with joy as I bring out the thermoses and huge flashlights from my bag. Marie had advised me to bring these to him for the annual fishing expedition about to take place.

"I am happy Marie Meade sent you here to learn about traditional birthing methods," Jo says, looking at his mother. "You must understand that our Inuit elders take time to thaw out. They have very strict rules of behavior. Marie Meade has had more practice in forming relationships with Westerners. You must be patient.

Jo suggests that I come with him to a local ceremony taking place not far away. It is in memory of one of the elders who died during the winter. "Until Mom will agree to speak with you about birth, you can learn about our rites of death. What do you think?" I am thrilled at the invitation. Jo loads up the ATV with equipment, blankets, pickaxes and crates of beer and soft drinks. He looks me up and down and says, "Not enough."

"Not enough?" I ask from under a sweater, coat, scarves, hat, gloves, boots and long johns. "Not enough," he insists, and puts another coat over me and a hat that covers my face except for my eyes. I can barely breathe and feel like a clumsy bear, but I climb into the ATV and we ride to the marina where large motorboats are docked.

About 30 men and women dressed in thick coats are loading things onto the boats. The atmosphere is hustle and bustle with a barrage of English and some throaty Yupik thrown in. Eyes peer at me out of the slots made by the hats and face masks. Jo explains to the curious crowd that I am from Israel and was sent by Marie Meade. The eyes seem to bulge a bit at this and I think I can see smiles behind scarves.

Our rocking boat holds eight people, and another four boats start up and we are on our way. I have no idea where. The boat carves a white foamy trail through the water and I hold on to whatever I can. The movement of the boat is not rough, but I have very little sailing experience. Jo steers with one hand. He looks every inch the strong and sure Chief Skipper. He knows which tributary of the river to go down and every tree along the way.

I have never felt cold like this in my life. I see why Jo bundled me up so much, but the wind still manages to creep in under all the layers. When he sees my eyes tearing up from the cold he signals me to move behind him. The other men understand and block me from the biting wind. One of the women puts a blanket around my shoulders.

We are surrounded by the expanse of the river, the noise of the motor, and the sound of the wind blowing through the huge white trees standing along the riverbank. A young man who is beside me waves his hand in the direction of the trees and points out the teeth marks of the beavers on the large trunks. Some of these great trees have not withstood the gnawing of the small animals and have fallen into the brush. Now I see a beaver gnawing a tree trunk and Jo tells me that they use the logs to create dams. Alongside the dams they will make safe homes in which to raise their young.

I see eagles circling above their nests and frightened ducks running for cover. A huge brown grizzly bear lumbers along the far bank of the river. I listen and stare at the great forests and the winding river, which seems to go on forever. Skipper Jo's hand is sure on the helm as he guides the wheel left and right towards our destination. I wonder how he can know exactly where to sail, as it all looks the same to me.

At one of the bends in the river a group of around 20 boats is gathered. We slow down, draw near and lay anchor. Everyone gets out of the boats onto the shore and greets one another happily. Giving big bear hugs, patting each other on the back, rubbing noses, and shaking hands encased in thick gloves.

Jo explains to me that the Yupik have special permission to fish a certain quota of the salmon that return every summer to their place of birth. Every tribal elder has a spot on the riverbank where he will go with his friends and family for a month at the end of June, or whenever the salmon return. The elder whom we are gathered here to honor and remember at this ceremony, who has passed from this world to the next, requested to be laid to rest here, at his fishing site. This is on condition that the summer comes and the land defrosts. On the shore stands a forlorn hut that contains some winter equipment.

These gatherings rarely take place because of the vast distances and difficult routes involved. They are a wonderful opportunity to talk, tell stories, and pass on information and gossip. Rumors of bears, changes in the river, weather conditions, how and when the supply barges arrive from the big city. Some houses in the region have satellite phones and some even have Internet and TV, but nothing beats a face to face, even when the faces are swathed in protective layers against the cold.

A large hole is dug in the earth. The local priest lights incense and waves it in big circles. The holy scent of the incense mingles with the clean smell of the trees. The priest wears a large cross on his chest. I look at the people around me. They are a mixture of Slavic, Russian and Inuit. They have square faces with pronounced chins and slightly slanted eyes. Among the almost 80 people present are representatives of each village in the region, all standing and praying.

I stand in the forest among them and listen to their prayers honoring the soul of the respected elder. They lower the casket into the hole, and the group files silently into the hut. It smells green and damp, like the forest. In the clean air only the popping of the pinecones and the chirping of birds can be heard.

In the hut the feast begins. Someone introduces herself to me as Katya, and invites me to eat. There is much to choose from: beaver meat, whale blubber, rice with forest grains, salads from local greens, potatoes that are worth their weight in gold, and of course salmon and many other fish dishes. The women gather round me, each offering tips about salmon. Everyone has their own family recipe handed down from the salmon-smoking elders. Salmon is a large part of Inuit culture.

Katya explains how the salmon swim enormous distances to reach streams of warm water in winter. When the short summer comes, they return to their place of origin, which is here in the tributaries of this area, and here the females lay their eggs. Their journey is long and full of perils. Some salmon will be eaten by the giant grizzlies who stand in the water and catch them with their paws. Others will end their lives in the nets of the Inuit elders who sweep them from the water. Katya explains that every old or middle-aged woman here has brought her own particular type of fish dish to this gathering. Tough competition.

Jo tells me that there is an elderly midwife present and perhaps I would like to speak with her. He points her out and I go and introduce myself. Her name is Alexandra. She is very happy to meet me and excited to hear that I come from Israel. She and most of her friends are evangelists. They are followers of the Old Testament and consider Israeli Jews to be God's chosen people. They believe that the establishment of the State of Israel on its ancient land is a fulfilment of biblical prophecy and proof of the covenant between God and his subjects. She touches my hand with deep emotion when I tell her that I grew up in Jerusalem, and asks me to describe Jerusalem and Bethlehem. After I tell her a little, I explain to her my purpose in visiting Alaska. Her eyes become cold. She says she does not know anything.

"Maybe you know someone who knows something about traditional birthing?"

She thinks for a minute and waves her hand at another woman. I go over to her. Same questions, same answers. She knows nothing. This happens quite a few times, until I begin to doubt my communication skills. What is going on here? The people are so friendly and continue to ask me about Israel and about Jesus. But as soon as I mention my reasons for coming here, they clam up.

In the afternoon, the cold becomes even colder. People start to leave and everyone wants to take a photograph with me. The cold sun continues to light up the sky. It will fade only at midnight and even then it will not be dark, only less light.

We begin to sail back.

At home, at dinner, Pala is no more amiable but she does ask me about Anchorage, and how the clouds looked from the plane. At the funeral, I was also asked several times about the clouds. I suppose that a lot of information can be gleaned from clouds about expected rain, snow, and wind. The weather here is changeable and flights in and out of the region are often cancelled, and plans must be altered suddenly. My time here is limited because my transatlantic flight from Anchorage is already fixed.

Toward the end of the meal the phone rings. When Jo returns to the table he informs me with quiet excitement that Katya, whom I met at the funeral, has invited me to her house for a sauna.

"It is not usual for a stranger to be invited to something like that. It must be because Marie sent you, or because you are from Israel." He explains this to me, but maybe also to himself and Pala.

The next afternoon Pala's daughter Maria escorts me to Katya's home in the neighborhood. We go around the back of the house to a small wooden building. There is a stack of firewood next to the door, which opens into a vestibule where we change our shoes to the plastic slippers. Another door opens into a small space with wooden walls and benches. There we get undressed. There is no embarrassment; this is a purely functional form of undressing.

It is nice and warm here, and we each get three towels. Maria explains the ritual. "When we enter the sauna we sit on one towel and with the other we soap ourselves. The towel for drying we leave with the clothes hanging up." The third and final door opens into the hot sauna. They signal me to enter and close the door so the steam won't escape. Maria and I sit down next to Katya and her daughter Sasha. Suddenly the door bursts open and an enormous and naked Pala steps in.

Steam fills the space and I sit naked on the wooden bench with four other women in a cloud of heat. All of our body fat rolls and folds. I observe the others carefully and try to do as they do. I am careful not to stare or meet any eyes, to be modest, quiet, and smile often. The space is small. On the floor near the benches are plastic mats. In the center a small round low metal box holds the sizzling red coals. Maria sits close to the container and every so often lifts one of the wide bowls of water next to her and pours it over the hot coals. There are other bowls with heated water for pouring over ourselves before and after soaping.

Every afternoon in the village, women meet and bathe in this manner. The ritual lasts about two hours, and in the pleasant and comforting heat the tribal status of a woman is decided. Intricate politics of who invited whom, and which social combinations are formed today because of yesterday, and so on. The conversation moves between Yupik and American English.

Behinds become striped from the benches, all the bumps and wrinkles on our bodies are exposed. Our breasts are flattened or plump, with dark nipples or light, wide or pert. Our stomachs … are a story unto themselves. Somehow here, in the damp air, completely

62

naked, Paula turns to me and begins to talk. Before she gets to the subject I am so curious to learn about, she speaks with sadness about the reality of life in the region.

The young people have nothing to do here and that boredom leads them to addictions of one kind or another and to babies born to young girls. In almost every home here you will find a baby being raised by a grandmother, as if it were her own child. If the young boy or girl has any problem at all with the authorities, they are put in jail straight away. The youth get in trouble because of drugs or alcohol. The American police have no patience for our youth. The only ones who escape this fate are the ones who find government jobs, which give them relative financial security.

"You, the strangers," she says while lathering her huge stomach, "think we live in igloos. I can't even remember what an igloo looks like. True, I did hunt whales. That was a necessity in times when food was scarce. We needed the blubber for nourishment to survive. The conditions here, despite modernization, are very harsh and very little remains of our heritage.

Maria pours water on the coals and white clouds rise up from the hot iron and spread throughout the small room. The women are listening to Pala and nod their heads in agreement.

"I always worked very hard, even when I was pregnant. My mother would tell me not to carry heavy things, but I had no choice. We have some very strict rules about behavior during pregnancy. In the morning a pregnant woman must get up, no lying around, and leave the house directly. Never mind the weather. They must go out the door without pausing on the threshold."

Maria nods at her mother. "When I was pregnant with my fourth daughter, I learned that lesson the hard way," she says. "Every morning I would get out of bed, go in the direction of the door and purposely stand in the doorway. My father was startled anew every morning. 'Maria,' he would say, 'be careful, that is dangerous.'

"When it came time for my delivery, here in the village, in the small birthing center, it was winter. The birth was progressing smoothly until I began pushing. The baby crowned and then returned inside! Again and again. I pushed for a long time until that little one managed to come out. Since then, I realized that we should listen to our elders.

"The words of the elders are important not only because they say so, but because all the generations they carry within them say so."

"Yes," Pala agrees, her skin reddish from the heat. "These are ancient beliefs. When we come out of the door quickly we are teaching the baby to act without hesitation. We learned this from our elders. The elders are with us and so is the baby in our womb. He knows, he hears and he learns."

There are other rules. Pregnant women are not allowed to eat leftovers from someone else's plate. If someone does, the baby will lack something. She shows me her hand, which is missing one finger. "Yes," she stresses dramatically, "It's true, and also," she continues, "eating whale blubber is important because it will supply the baby and the mother with good energy."

Everyone nods in agreement.

How is it that here, in the sauna, I have managed to overcome the hurdle that the Alaskan women had placed in front of me? Perhaps the nakedness has blurred the differences between us? I want to ask a few questions but am afraid to break the trust that has finally been awarded to me. In the end, I do dare to ask about the behavior of the older women at the ceremony yesterday.

Did they really not know about birthing?

Pala frowns, but Maria answers. "The tribal elders have a lot of power. They own the fishing rights and the land. Our rules of behavior demand that we just listen to the elders without opening our mouths and without asking questions."

Now I understand that I had crossed a red line. The fact that I asked direct questions was a threat to their social structure. This wasn't the first time that I could not control myself when visiting different cultures. Rather than waiting patiently for the social codes to be revealed to me, I was anxious to know and to explore, so I was not very polite. In the eyes of the locals I am seen as inconsiderate and rude.

In South Dakota, for example, it was accepted behavior for people taking part in the Sun Dance not to pay for food or lodging. Instead, everyone donated whatever amount they saw fit. I wanted to do something different, and offered to cook an Israeli-style lunch. The suggestion was brought before the manager of the kitchen, Katerina, a 45-year-old Lakota woman. She had been a radical lawyer who fought for the right of Native American people to return to their lands. She was also renowned as a brave hunter who had lived with the wolves on the outskirts of the reservation.

Not the kind of person you would like to have as your enemy.

Katerina accepted my request and helped me to quantify how much of each ingredient I would need to cook for 300 people. Full of enthusiasm, I enlisted some friends to help alongside the appointed kitchen crew. We made lentil soup for starters, along with Israeli salad and a burghul? with tahini dish. I had seen Katerina preparing the rest of the meal, but to my great surprise only what I had prepared was served. It was well received, but was not nearly enough. Everyone was left hungry I felt very embarrassed.

At first I could not understand why Katerina would do such a thing, but afterwards, when my anger subsided, I understood that

I had trampled upon her territory, her kitchen, and her position as nurturer of the tribe. She had decided to punish my rude behavior and to teach me a lesson about manners in a strange place..

The next day I gave her a nice present I had brought from Israel, and thanked her from the bottom of my heart for the honor she had bestowed upon me. I also thanked her for the lesson in humbling myself that she had taught me. I realized that I had much to learn about approaching societies whose rules I do not know. I understood that I must be much more patient.

After a long silence, Katya speaks. It is difficult for me to understand her English, and the sounds seem to come from deep in her throat.

"I was born in the far North in a very isolated place, more isolated than this village. I do not know in which month of the pregnancy I was born, but I was very small. Soon after the birth, my grandfather went out to hunt and came back with a whale which was still warm. My grandfather dug deep into the whale, wrapped me in soft furs and placed me inside the whale."

Like a huge, living incubator, I thought to myself.

"Because I was so small, my grandmother would boil frozen salmon, dip a feather into the fat and give it to me to suck on. Like a natural incubator. She did this for a few weeks, until I was strong enough to nurse on my own. And here, you see?" She announces proudly, "Here I am, and I have my own children and grandchildren."

Her daughter Sasha nods. "Yes," she says, "but there were many who died. That is how it was. Whoever died, led those who came after."

I am glad to see that my direct question did not stop the conversation. There were many twists and turns to it. Like the gradual entrances to the homes here. A vestibule leads to another room and into another, and at every stage you must take something off in order to enter the next stage, until finally you enter the house. Like the layers of clothing that one must put on to protect against the cold and then shed to enter the sauna. Now, I sit naked with other naked women and finally hear what I came to hear about.

Before I began my journey to Alaska I knew that the penetration into this cold region which is so isolated and vulnerable would be difficult, but I didn't realize how difficult. I did not predict one fundamental hitch – that they would not want to share their knowledge with a stranger. I did not even understand what it was that I did not understand.

The moment I was admitted into the warm, soft, and accepting womb of the sauna was the moment when I passed the test of approval. After that, even when I asked a question that perhaps I should not have, the conversation continued. This makes me very happy and calms me.

I am wrapped in a towel, the steamy heat is lovely, and the conversation goes on until we dress and exit into the cold outside

Two days later I return to Anchorage. I am sitting in Marie's kitchen and telling her about what happened in the village. She is glad to hear that I managed to break through the barriers and learned something about traditional birth from the elders.

Marie continued to teach me customs and traditions around pregnancy and birth. She explained to me how to speak to the baby. "The baby hears everything and must be included in whatever is going on," she says. "The baby is a conscious being already in the womb. You must talk to him so that he will feel secure and so that he will learn." Marie lifts up the collar of her shirt with two hands and hides her mouth inside to show me how to speak to the baby. "Closely and quietly." She tells me that her father was a shaman, and already in the womb knew whatever was happening to his mother. He would see what she ate and what she experienced. He could feel all her energies during the pregnancy.

"A woman must not drink a lot, only when she is thirsty." Marie repeats what Katya had said in the sauna about eating leftovers, but her explanation is different. "An expectant mother must under no circumstances eat leftovers. Eating only a part of something will teach the baby that there are parts, and we want the baby to learn to be whole. That everything he does he will do with his whole self."

Katya spoke about physical wholeness and Marie about wholeness of spirit. They both told me that during and after birthing, it is important to give the birth mother whale blubber for strength. During the initiation ceremony they dress the baby warmly in soft furs and take him out into the snow. They place him on the path that leads to the house and roll him until he arrives at the doorway. This rite symbolizes the continuously revolving wheel of life. He is now blessed to roll successfully throughout his life.

Marie arranges a going-away party for me. Grandmother Rita Pitka Blumenstein is present, as is her granddaughter who will carry on her grandmother's wisdom. Marie's daughters and granddaughters are here and many friends and neighbors. The table is full of local refreshments. Grandmother Rita smiles at me and gestures me to approach her. She is sitting on the couch and I kneel to her. She holds my face in her hands, giggling, and says some sentences in Yupik. While she continues to gaze deep into my eyes she says that she and her ancestors wish me a good life. She bends towards me and hugs me, kisses me on the lips, and tells me Shalom in Hebrew.

After my return to Israel, someone told me a story about a researcher who arrived in Alaska and made an appointment with a man from the Yupik Tribe. The Yupik said he would be happy to meet with her the next day, but the next day he left on a fishing expedition which lasted several weeks. The researcher interviewed various other residents of the tribe and came to the conclusion that the tribal peoples of the Arctic Circle, North America and Canada do not plan for tomorrow as do Westerners.

To them, the future is not a piece of time which can be captured. Life simply unfolds, and no one can dictate how it will unfold. The present, past and future are all taking place at once, and souls continue to exist at all times and in all dimensions. The soul's incarnation may not be the same in the past as in the future, but it continues to exist nevertheless.

Now I am better able to understand Grandmother Rita's answer to me on the way to the ceremony .She had said that she knows the correct treatment for each man or woman only when she meets them, in real time, face to face.

I remember her speaking about Yupik views on death. The Yupik see death as an inseparable part of life. Not as an end, or even as a break, but rather as a move into another dimension. The dead are seen as continuing to be part of the lives of the living. Even if a baby dies during birth he will be a part of present lives. Although it is a sad event, the belief that he was alive in the past and will exist (perhaps in another form) in the future is comforting and enables people to cope better with loss.

The theme which unified all of my Alaskan experiences was 'passageways' – the in-between zones which lead to new and different territory. My bumpy plane ride, my freezing sailing trip. The funeral rite of passage near the river, the vestibules leading into the homes and the sauna, my own personal transition from complete stranger to an accepted person in Yupik society.

In order to be admitted to a different society I had to forget all

I knew, to give up my own expectations and plans which I had set before coming. I was greatly distressed when I realized that in spite of the huge effort I had made to come there, the results were not at all what I had expected.

Only upon my return to Israel did I understand the connections between what I had undergone and other passages I had been through in my lifetime. The road the old women had led me on was similar to the road on which a human being travels when he or she passes through unexpected experiences and achieves a different status. The feelings of insecurity that accompany almost all changes in life, increase while you are going through the process and the various unknowns that feature in it.

The human brain wants to clearly divide experiences into categories like bad and good, life and death, woman and man, high and low, defiled and pure, etc. This duality gives man a feeling of security and order. He is uncomfortable when things are not categorized or will not fit into orderly opposites. Whenever we are at mid-stage, about to transition from one identity to another, it will feel threatening and scary at some level.

Rites of passage were created to help us cope with these feelings of insecurity and undermined identity. In every age and in every culture these rituals exist. They accompany an array of situations. Their function is to help us process the changes occurring and to reduce the stress that they cause. Whether it is changes of season, changes within the social order, or changes of a personal nature. In every rite of passage, three stages are clearly identifiable.

The first is detachment and separation from one's present status. The person must shed his identity and prepare to change. The separation will be demonstrated by the use of specific actions and symbolic rituals, such as in Judaism, when the hair of an ultra-Orthodox boy will be cut for the first time at the age of three. He is now separated from his infancy and will be advancing into boyhood.

The second stage is transition. At this stage, a person has left his old position but has not yet entered into the new one. This in-between stage is often characterized by uncertainty and ambiguousness. One's new personal identity is not yet achieved and there is a period of disorientation. The normal boundaries of thought and behavior are stretched and relaxed. This liminal stage usually includes physical challenges. For example, in traditional societies young men are required to undergo grueling hardships in order to be considered men. A woman must undergo the pains of childbirth in order to become a mother.

The final stage is incorporation and acceptance of the new role. This is often accompanied by the use of sacred items. At graduation from college, a cap and gown are worn. At the time of marriage, vows and rings are exchanged.

Birth is a critical juncture and full of meaning in the life of a human being. It contains the potential for both the giving and loss of life. It is a situation in which reality is shaken to its core: what has been will no longer be, the known will vanish, and the participants all stand at the threshold of a new phase in their lives.

In every society, throughout time, various rituals are performed to herald the birth of a new baby into the world and to celebrate the transformation of a woman into a mother. At every birth, all three stages are fully represented.

The mother-to-be sheds her principal identity, and will no longer be described in the same way that she was before the birth. This shedding requires entering into a state of consciousness which relaxes her normal boundaries of behavior. She is not conscious of time and space as we know it when she enters into her trance of birthing.

The wild, primal side of her nature takes over. The limbic parts of her brain are in control and will order her body to secrete opiate hormones. In a very real way she has shed her previous guise, and has now partially or completely exposed her primal mode of being.

This stage can be recognized by her intensity of emotion and wild stormy feelings. By her screams during childbirth and statements such as she "wants to die." During this transitional phase of the birth process, when the cervix is completely open, many women feel that it is the "end of the world," "I cannot go on," "Help me." These cries come from the depths of her soul, and symbolically she **is** going to die. Her identity as she knew it will disappear and a new being will emerge – a mother.

The baby also sheds his previous condition and during this same rite of passage will become redefined. From a fetus, he transforms into a newborn.

After the birth, a long period of adjustment begins. The baby will get used to life outside the womb little by little. His bodily functions will mature and adjust themselves to his new reality. His digestive system (the functioning of which is not fully formed in the womb) must become more stabilized and build up bacterial flora. The respiratory system, blood clotting mechanism, temperature regulation and other physiological systems must all become more firmly established. His motor abilities and his emotional abilities, such as judgment and socializing, are all just beginning to organize.

At the same time that he is adjusting to all these changes he is also becoming a social member of society. He enters into a specific family, to specific parents. He is written into the registry of the community as the son or daughter of these parents, and is now considered a member of society. He is assigned a first and last name and has rights and duties.

The new mother, meanwhile, is also undergoing a process of adjustment and building her new identity. Sometimes this is a smooth transition and sometimes it is difficult, and can even cause her to lose her sanity. Many Western women describe this period as very challenging. The loss of sleep, the physical changes to their bodies, the demands of nursing, the symbiosis with the baby, all these elements can be hard to get used to and take a long time to balance.

All women must adjust to their new role as a Mother in all human societies.

Among the Yupik these three stages also take place, and the mother prepares for her transformation ahead of time, during the pregnancy. The ceremony I described above, in which the pregnant woman must wake up in the morning and immediately leave her house, is a ritual designed to help her cope with the upcoming changes. It is a symbolic yet useful practice that gives her a feeling of control over a process which is by nature quite beyond control. The future mother prepares herself and the baby she carries to make the passage in a useful fashion. In the third stage of accepting the new position, the Yupiks roll the baby in the snow to bless him with a long and successful journey on the wheel of life

In Alaska, I personally experienced a different way of looking at time and space. The present moment was not static but circular, and contained also the past and the future. Because a circle has no high or low point, no start or finish, the dual way of thinking that I was accustomed to was no longer useful. For me, this allowed my movements through the passages to be calmer and I was more easily able to accept changes.

The rite of passage that turns a woman into a mother and a fetus into a baby seemed more diffused in their culture, not so drastic.

The shedding of a previous persona for an old Yupik woman,

for example, takes place inside a sphere where there are other souls to guide her. According to their view, souls are eternal and pass on through the generations. A fetus is already a fully conscious being who can see and hear all that goes on (although as if he were under ice). This is what they say, and since pain and suffering are a part of this eternal wheel of existence they can accept it with understanding.

In the techno-modern society, the rite of passage also occurs within a specific socio-cultural network. There are sub-rituals which symbolize the passage, and rules created that put emphasis on practicality and control over the birthing mother. The birth takes place in a delivery room. By various means (of which only a few are clinically based), the hospital creates an environment for the rite of passage which is completely cleansed of any personal characteristics of the birthing mother. She is cut off from her normal surroundings and from any symbols or signs of her individual character.

She is required to take off her own clothes and change into a hospital gown. This is a uniform, exactly like everyone else's, and blurs the differences between her and any other woman. She will be treated according to her identity number, or room number, or the number rating her progress of dilation. She will be hooked up to the pipeline of the system – the drip (whether open or closed) – and to the monitor. The system and its people now have her under control for the remainder of her passage.

The system has turned the birth mother into a passive player in her own rite of passage. She must lie down; her body is penetrated. She must follow orders and relinquish control of the entire process to the medical staff. Sometimes this is what the birth mother wants and at times it's done against her will. Sometimes this situation is helpful and at times not.

Take, for example, a birth mother who has been in labor for many hours, but is told that her cervical dilation is still small. She will lose faith in herself and in the natural process. She would have to know that the amount of cervical dilation is only one factor among many which indicate how the birth is progressing, and is actually the least relevant in predicting this.

In any case, the birth mother is ripped from the fabric of her normal life and her identity as an individual, and her ability to choose or make decisions about her own labor becomes extremely limited. The medical staff take control over the rite of passage. The standardized regulations and procedures cancel out all of her personal preferences and beliefs that have meaning for her and substitute a cold, alienating, and flat experience. Some of the rules and policies in delivery rooms are not based on any medical considerations and some will even increase the suffering of the birth mother in her time of passage.

A woman who must lie down on her back so that the heartbeat of the fetus can be monitored will suffer more than a woman who is allowed to lie or move in a way that her body dictates. She should have freedom of movement, so that the baby can position itself correctly in her pelvic region. Lying down also puts pressure on her tailbone and aggravates pains during contractions. The tailbone should be free to move during the birth to create space within the pelvis and widen it internally.

The professional medical staff undoubtedly believe that this is the correct way for the rite of passage to unfold. They believe that it is only about complying with required safety precautions, even though delivery room protocols vary in different countries and hospitals. And there are enough of these protocols to prove it is likely that some other solutions are possible under the same circumstances.

For example, the way of relating to a delivery according to

pre-determined parameters. The progress of the birth used to be measured by Friedman's Curve. This measures the widening of the cervix at the rate of 1 centimeter per hour. Recently, however, the WHO changed its stance on the relevance of the curve for determining preparedness for labor.

In short, the staff do not attempt to analyze the individual's advancement according to her natural processes. The handling of the delivery is based on an *estimate* of the baby's weight. It can have a 10% to 20% margin in each direction. This means that a baby estimated to be 6.6 lbs. can be born with a weight between 5.5 and 7.5 lbs. method of basing the decisions about delivery on an estimated weight (for example, recommending Cesarean section if the weight is over 9.9 lbs.) is not consistent and differs among delivery rooms and medical personnel. Recording the heartbeat of the fetus is another factor that can be interpreted in completely different ways depending on the views of the medical team involved and their personal experience.

All of these different factors are used to create statistics that falsify information even more.

I feel that the following questions beg to be asked:

Is there a way in which traditional birth, honoring the creation of life and respectful of this spiritual and cultural rite of passage, can be interwoven with modern techno birth procedures that regard safety and science as central elements of a birth?

Why do modern women acquiesce to being controlled and acted upon even in their finest hour? Why do they agree to be turned into controllable objects by those whose main objective is not in their own best interest?

Wouldn't it be possible to have a situation where the birthing mother can feel protected medically and still have control over her own intimate process? Where the birth can be safe and the needs of the birth mother protected as well? Isn't it possible to find a way to listen to the baby's heartbeat while still allowing the birth mother to concentrate on herself and to move according to her internal rhythm?

Medical centers can easily provide these options. The rite of passage can be carried out and the safety of the baby and mother assured at the same time.. This possibility can be taken into hospital delivery rooms even when there is a need for technological intervention. Here, too, it is possible to decrease the birthing mother's fear about what is happening inside her, to safeguard her individuality and continue to treat the delivery with respect as a rite of passage, and still allow her to go through the process as she sees fit.

When the mother is in this very vulnerable situation, in limbo between one stage and the next, she is fearful and in pain. Her self-confidence is low and she doubts her own ability. It is then very easy to influence her to act in accordance with the methods suggested by the medical staff around her. But later, when she is through the process and her fears have faded away, she is likely to review the events with sorrow and feel that she was swept along in a direction that was not really what she wanted.

If the participants in the room – the woman in labor, the midwife, the doctors and nurses – all understood that the birth is not merely a physical event, but is the most important human rite of passage, they could all act appropriately.

If the woman was permitted to take responsibility for her own decisions, the ritual could proceed according to her wishes. Just as a couple plan their wedding ceremony according to their individual priorities and beliefs, the mother and parents-to-be should be allowed to choose to whom she or they entrust the management of the birth ceremony.

If midwives understood the importance of this process, this special moment when the gates of heaven open and a new soul comes into this world, they would act with care and sensitivity – not only as midwives, but as guides and supervisors of the rite of passage.

If hospitals would allow the mother-to-be to decorate and organize the delivery room as she wishes (music, scents, ornaments) and to wear what she likes (or nothing at all), and allow her to perform rituals of her choice, be they prayer, chanting, etc. then her individuality will not be erased

Even if the woman chooses to use a form of pain relief, the delivery room can still be sacrosanct. Even with an epidural administered, the process is still physically and spiritually demanding and in the end the transformation into motherhood takes place. When the ritual is performed the way the woman chooses and by people who know what she is asking for, who know what she believes in and what is important to her, she will give birth with confidence, and her new identity as a mother will emerge in a much more whole way along with that of her infant.

Over Denalay Mountain

On the river

Kaligonak Village

Grandma Rita Pitka

Madagascar - Aren't They in Pain?

The young woman in labor crouches on the bed. Her face is taut with effort, her lips slightly parted as she quietly pants and pushes. Outside the door children are playing, and smoke from the cooking fire sneaks in the open window. Chickens cackle and women chat in Malagasy mixed with French. The women laugh and smile as they bustle about the room. One folds a sheet, one checks the baby clothes prepared on the bed, another one enters with a large plastic cup full of steaming hot water for the woman in labor, who meanwhile – labors.

I arrived in Madagascar a month before Riva's labor began. I had a long flight with stopovers in Ethiopia and South Africa before landing in Antananarivo, the capital city. What first caught my attention was the large number of children everywhere. The littlest ones were held in arms or tied on backs, tied somehow to someone. The ones who were a bit bigger were roaming around freely. One child holds a plate of food and puts rice into his mouth with his hand. A colorful bird distracts him and wonderment causes him to run and try to catch its tail. The plate is forgotten, or maybe not, and so the day passes. The bigger children look after the smaller ones. No adult watches over them.

This is very different from what I am used to. In my country children must be protected every minute from catastrophes such as eating nuts or hot dogs, germs and dirt. I was amazed to see children running among the green hills with no teacher and no fear, chasing after a piece of colored cellophane flashing and flying in the wind,

After a few days in the capital I travel eastward. Madagascar is an island off the eastern coast of Africa and to its east lie two other smaller islands, which are often swept by hurricanes. In a long canoe I sail to one of them, called Ile aux Nattes.

Rinanzaza Jeanette, the midwife, is full of smiles and energy as she massages Riva. She concentrates mostly on the region of her thighs and groin. After a while she helps Riva to get up and go outside. I go out with them into the dappled sun and shadow of the jungle surrounding the clinic. In the backyard, Jeanette takes off all of Riva's clothes. The young woman's oily black body gleams in the sunbeams which dance over her large breasts and buttocks. She crouches down and leans against a tree trunk.

Jeanette pours water on her from a green plastic pitcher. The water runs down her body and the midwife strokes her gently. She speaks soft and honeyed words of endearment and encouragement, telling Riva that it will only be a little bit longer and her baby will soon be here.

In Malagasy, *rinanzaza* means midwife; *rinan* means mother and *zaza* means baby. The midwife's work is considered important enough for her to be thought of as the mother to each baby she delivers.

Rinanzaza Jeanette is a small and cheerful 45-year-old woman. Two ponytails curl on either side of her face and both her nose and mouth are wide. She is descended from a family of midwives, and from as far back as she can remember she joined her mother in caring for women in childbirth,

I had visited her in her home the day before Riva's birthing. In her garden, lettuce grew in the sunshine along with flowers, bushes and other vegetables. Cats and chickens roamed the yard, and in the distance I could see the sea washing over whales and dolphins. The jungle is close by, teeming with life. Lemur monkeys chatter among the branches and vanilla vines climb up the tree trunks. In this season, the vanilla pods are green and the scent is intoxicatingly sweet. Millions of birds chirp from the treetops. Large ferns and lush plants intertwine in the humid air.

At the entrance to Jeanette's house stand cages containing hamsters, rabbits and guinea pigs. All these animals are used as food here. She runs a tight ship at home and her daughter stands in the kitchen frying little doughnuts. The warm scent of oil and sugar fills the air. Births usually take place in Jeanette's house, but this time it is in the clinic.

"Why is the birth in the clinic?" I ask in broken French mixed with English and a lot of hand movements. "Why not in your house?"

She says that the clinic is safer because this birth may be more complicated than usual. Complicated births are usually relegated to the big medical center which is a few hours from here by boat. This time they decided that there wasn't enough time for that. According to surveys done by the CIA, in Madagascar 42 out of every 1,000 infants will die during their first year of life, so the fear of losing your baby in childbirth here is very real. In spite of this, Jeanette, and every midwife I spoke with in Madagascar, told me that they had never had any problems during deliveries.

The clinic staff consists of Jeanette, her son Uvi (who is the village doctor), and the village women who come to assist at birthings. After her shower in the yard the mother-to-be is wrapped in a green cloth and we return inside. Jeanette now puts a midwife glove on one hand and a white apron. When she takes care of Riva she covers her mouth with a medical mask.

Dr. Uvi explains that from his palpitation of the belly he has determined that the baby is large and to be on the safe side, the birth will require Pitocin to bring on the labor. This is exactly what is done in our modern delivery rooms – taking care of a possible problem before it occurs. I begin to suspect that it is important for them to convince me that they meet Western standards for hygiene. The two of them are putting on a show to impress me. They measure the belly with a tailor's tape measure and listen to the baby's heartbeat with a little trumpet-shaped instrument. After the young doctor listens gravely, he straightens up and with a smile of victory announces that all is well.

I realize now for certain that my presence is influencing 'the field.' When a foreign anthropologist arrives on a scene 'the field' will react and behave differently. I am a foreign element, and will never know what would have happened if I was not here. Probably the birth would have taken place in the midwife's house, like most of them. Perhaps there is not even any danger of complication, they just want to show off their professional Western knowledge. Here, Western doctors and White Man in general are considered godlike and all-knowing. Because of this belief they are all too quick to relinquish their traditional practices.

The birth continues to unfold rhythmically to the pleasant sound of the rain outside. The young woman is in deep inward concentration as she walks comfortably about the room. She circles the bed, leans on the rusty windowsill and breathes. She does not utter any sound, not a peep.

In Madagascar everything seems to happen slowly. Their speech is slow. Their whole culture seems to advocate length as a virtue.

People speak with pauses between words and even inside words. A long aaaaah fills in the spaces. It seems that speech has succumbed to the languidness of the place. The words themselves are very long and melodic, and speaking is like a long, soft, exhalation of aaaah which continues on and on. When I say out loud the name of the capital, Aantaanaarrrivoo, time seems to stretch endlessly before me.

It did not happen immediately, but after a short while in Madagascar I fell in love with the tempo, the smells, the houses made of red earthen bricks. I feel at peace here, where nothing is urgent and everything is already just as it should be. No comparisons or judgments, just living and experiencing.

There are humped cattle here called *zebu* that wander along serenely through the clear uncontaminated air. People smile at each other warmly. There is no Internet or telephone or haste. Even the cars drive slowly. Couples stroll in sync on the way to work and children wander and play. A not-so-young man is playing soft music on a simple sort of harp called a *vahila*.

Every road shown on the map as a highway turns out to be a narrow one-lane road that occasionally widens into two lanes. The bumpy roads, full of potholes, large cracks and ruts, wind through the beautiful scenery, causing everyone to slow down. Perhaps that is why there is time to smile. I am amazed at how in such conditions of extreme heat and cold, typhoons, thorns, and hard work bent over rice paddies – everyone smiles. Maybe in the hard barren desert of south Madagascar, where there is nothing, people smile less. But here they smile often and laugh out loud with wide-open mouths.

The mother of the woman in labor is also smiling as she offers her daughter a bowl full of rice and cassava leaf. She prepared it ahead of time and carried it in a straw basket to the clinic. In Madagascar, rice is the staple food and is very important. Three times a day a large pile of rice is heaped into a bowl. For lunch, a thick sauce containing green leaves of various kinds, beans, carrots, and pieces of meat or fish is poured over the rice. In the morning the rice can be diluted to make pap and sometimes sweetened. At every meal a large quantity of rice is consumed.

Jeanette says to me, "Rice helps the woman in childbirth," and explains that rice has many healing qualities. It is magical, brings blessings, and aids the birth process. The mother feeds her daughter a few spoonfuls of rice. The daughter continues to move slowly about the room. She leans forward and the midwife comes behind her to massage her back. I ask Jeanette what she does to ease the pains of labor.

"Childbirth does hurt," she answers, and then demonstrates on me the thigh massage she did on Riva. "I do this when the woman is tired." I enjoy the massage very much because I, too, am tired.

I have asked traditional midwives throughout the world how they help women to cope with the pain of childbirth, and my question is always met with a look of incomprehension, "Birth is painful," they answer, and that's it. Birthing mothers in Israel and elsewhere in the Western world are busy thinking about the pain long before the birth occurs. They are deciding whether to take an epidural or other form of pain relief; they practice breathing, massage, and other techniques intended to make the pain bearable.

Here in Madagascar, as in many places where life is lived mainly out of doors, alongside nature, and is affected by extremes of weather and hard physical labor, I feel that they really do not know what I am talking about when I ask about "The Pain" of childbirth. I have come to understand that the question I am asking is based on a cultural assumption. I assume it hurts, and therefore that something must be done about it.

I have decided that in Madagascar my research will be more focused on this subject. Does it hurt them? Maybe it hurts them less? How do they relate to pain? How does the attitude toward pain in traditional agrarian societies compare to the attitude toward pain in the modern world? Labor pains are the only physical pains in nature that are not connected to bodily harm. They do not occur in conjunction with any danger, wound, or disease.

Ruth Benedict, an American anthropologist born at the end of the nineteenth century, claimed that pain in general, and pains of labor specifically, are social concepts. The birthing mother in Madagascar responds to pain with self-control, whether it hurts a lot or a little.

In Japan, the births I have attended are very quiet and restrained. It was explained to me that this self-control stems from their cultural norm that it is not acceptable to show feelings in public. They believe that the only sounds that should be heard in a delivery room are the cries of the newborn. Muslim women, on the other hand, believe that screaming during labor will show God the Creator that women are paying for Original Sin.

Mindy Levi is a midwife in the organization "Ima" in Israel. She gives lectures on coping with pain to many groups of women. She found that in remote villages in India and Bangladesh, showing restraint during birthing is a sign of bravery and strength of character.

Among the women of the Hausa tribe of Nigeria, being quiet while giving birth is a sign of modesty. Other tribes in Nigeria teach their girls from a young age that it is shameful to show fear when having a baby.

Traditional midwives treat the pain as a fact of life. They are not concerned with making the pain go away, but see it as a normal and natural event. In the Western world we have managed to separate ourselves from our own bodies. We teach our bodies to behave as we want them to. They are not permitted to hurt, to smell, to fall apart, or to bother us in any way.

Companies were created to beautify and take care of our bodies so that we (and those around us) will not feel the changes taking place in them (such as old age or disease). We are very concerned with staying healthy. This stems from the wish to lengthen our lives as much as possible. Death for us is an end that nobody wants. Nowadays, death is thought of more and more often as a technical breakdown that can surely be fixed (as Yuval Harari states in his book, *A Brief History of Tomorrow*).

In the Western world a young, hale body signifies health and postponement of that final hour. Following this line of thinking, everything that reminds us of the body's fragility is pushed aside and removed from the public eye. Bodily secretions are dealt with only in private, bodily odors must be disguised and every effort is made to circumvent pain – even pain that we know is only temporary.

Using all his scientific powers, Western man struggles to keep at a distance anything that could be interpreted as a sign of disease, old age, or death. Therefore, his body can no longer effectively deal with physical hardship or pain. Whenever pain, heat, cold, weariness, etc. arises, it is interpreted as a warning sign of a problem that can and must be solved.

The fear of pain and resistance to the obvious fact of the body's impermanence form a very large part of Western culture. When we encounter pain, for instance during childbirth, it comes as a big surprise and we have no tools to cope with it. We see it as negative and as something we must eradicate, even though the experience as a whole is a positive one.

The silencing of our bodies has led us up to this point – where we cannot accept the pains of childbirth as a natural part of life. The body itself has regulatory mechanisms during the birth process. For example, hormones are secreted to diminish the pain. The body knows how to give birth, but the fear of pain that we have been taught to see as negative prevents us from connecting to the entire birth process. We cannot relax and reach the point in labor where our body will function naturally to relieve pain.

Riva climbs onto the bed, crouches, and begins to push. The major part of the effort seems to be in her face. She does not show any sign of pain. Everything in the room is relaxed, and the talking dies down. Once in a while one of the women says something and everyone laughs. The woman in labor does not complain.

This behavior is very different from that in delivery rooms in Israel, where in most cases the woman is very loudly expressing her discomfort.

Riva has been pushing now for some time and I am getting worried. She changes her position. Again she shifts. It is taking a long time. What if something is wrong? I am worried about the birth and more so because I suspect that because of my presence something has been altered in the delicate makeup of the birthing process. That my crass invasion into such a special and protected space has changed the balance that should have been here. These thoughts bother me. I am concerned that if something does go wrong, they will blame me and the bad luck I brought.

My worrying comes from my desire to control the birth and prevent a catastrophe. But when I look around I see that I am the only one who is stressed. Everyone else is going about their business, arranging, chatting, not seeming the least bit concerned.

This is a women's space. The atmosphere here contains ancient, intuitive wisdom, and the strong presence of the women who are physically here now as well as those who have been here before us. The space envelops and pacifies all tensions and fears. There is a solidarity here between the living and the dead who continue to help and advise. Death walks here alongside life. The women around me know death up close. The life expectancy here is not very long and they are exposed to death in their daily lives. The very widely held concept of continuity between life and death in this culture influences the atmosphere of peacefulness and acceptance at the birth.

I breathe together with the woman in childbirth. She is making an effort, pushing, and then we hear voices outside. Help has arrived! All eyes look toward the door and an old, old grandmother, all wrinkles and smiles, steps in. She brings hard new rice fresh from the fields, prayers whispered to the ancestors who are floating in this space unseen but fully felt. She mumbles long words, strews a handful of rice over the birthing mother, touches her, breathes in and out, touches her again and tosses another pinch of rice.

She blesses and smiles and recites long slow sentences to the congregation of women surrounding the birthing mother. The woman in labor opens her mouth and the old woman puts some uncooked rice in it. Riva chews and we can hear the sound of her teeth grinding the grains of rice. From this will come blessing.

On the bed, two tiny hats await the tender newborn. One is light blue and the other pink. They are prepared for both options.

The birth is not progressing and I begin to worry again. The others still look calm. They do not give fear as much weight or space as I do. They know that whatever will be, will be. Patience and endurance are the way of life here. I need to learn this from them. The people's gentle spirit is reflected in this delivery room. There is no sound of protest from the birth mother. Everything moves slowly and peacefully. The chickens roam about the room, the grandmother smiles, the doctor and young mothers come in and out with their babies tied to their backs with colorful cloths, and snot-nosed kids peek in from time to time

I try to breathe more slowly and to trust in the spirit of creation that this baby will come into the world safely and peacefully. Why should he hurry? I ask myself. He walked with his mother's slow steps while in the womb. He felt the sun rise slowly through the wall of her stomach. He smelled the smell of her womb and he heard the birds chirp and felt the waters of his home. The birthing mother pants harder and gives another long, long push and ... it's a girl!

There is laughter in the room and the new mother smiles as the sweat from her labor runs down her body. The baby rests between her legs and is beginning to breathe slowly. I am shaking. A new baby girl has arrived in this world, straight into the loving arms of all the village women here, and into blankets and winter clothes. Even in the middle of summer the new mother will also be wrapped in a thick woolen sweater, and have blankets piled on top of her and her head wrapped in a warm hat, so that she will stay healthy and be safe and protected from all harm.

I have come across this idea of keeping the new mother warm in other places, such as on the floating islands of Bolivia on Lake Titicaca. One midwife there told me that the new mother should stay in her hut for 40 days wrapped in many clothes, even during the hottest days of summer, and should not go out.

In Madagascar, the new mother will not eat vegetables after the birth, only cooked food, mainly meat, and certain types of shrimp that contain high amounts of protein and will help with milk production. There should be lots of ginger in all the dishes she eats. Chicken soup is good, and many warm drinks are also advisable. According to tradition, all these "warming" foods will help the new mother to stay warm, heal, and regain her strength.

The baby makes soft cries, while around her the hive buzzes with activity. One woman cleans, one wipes the baby, one bathes the mother and another fixes her a hot drink, Others are taking the bed outside to air, and all of this is done amid laughter, smiles and long drawn-out words.

Everything runs calmly and smoothly. The baby girl is wrapped up and lies next to her resting mother. Everything flows along slowly; there is no rushing about. There is no one who must be notified about the birth because the whole village knows already, and if someone did not yet hear, the fleet-footed children will skip down the lanes to tell of the newest member of their community.

Almost every female of the village was present at the birth at one time or another – the girls, babies, young women and old women. Births of babies, like the births of animals, are an everyday event, observed by all. That is why when the time comes for a woman to give birth herself, she knows what to expect. They are all familiar with the process, they know what it looks like, smells like, and what a woman will go through in order for the baby to be born.

Most women in the West never saw their friends or any animals give birth, and their first exposure to the smells, secretions, and physical aspect of the birthing process will be at their own baby's birth. TV reality shows about childbirth portray only modern Western delivery rooms. Here, birth is almost always considered to be a medical procedure requiring professional medical intervention, with pain as the central theme. The suffering of the woman in childbirth and the possibilities of decreasing her pain are the focus of the show. This serves to reinforce the existing doctrine of the Western world towards birthing.

These shows never reveal that these delivery rooms are foreign to the woman in childbirth. That they isolate her from her known world. That the medical team does not know her or her family. That the staff speak among themselves in a jargon that she does not understand. That there is no attention paid to her feelings of alienation, which are only worsened if this is her first experience of a birth. All these factors reduce her ability to cope with pain and to relax.

True, in the last few years a woman is permitted to bring her husband, mother, doula or friend into the delivery room. This *does* help her to feel more protected, but is still a far cry from the experience in the clinic of the Malagasy mother, who goes through the birth surrounded by women she has known all her life, giving her support and comfort.

The women that I accompany as a doula *know* that birth is a normal, healthy process, but their short-term experience of this that they have with me cannot prepare them sufficiently for the attack on their senses that occurs in the delivery room. Fear of the intense pain becomes a self-feeding circuit. Fear leads to tension and tension increases the pain. Many women want to prevent the pain, and the medical system, which considers the pain to be "unhealthy" encourages the women and their families to "take an epidural" because why should you be in pain? And they call women "primitive" for even considering going through the natural pains of labor.

The French obstetrician Frédérick Leboyer developed the idea that it is possible to bring children into the world in a gentle fashion. He wrote the book *Birth Without Violence* in which he describes how a woman who is scared and tense causes her body to secrete stress hormones, which in turn restrict oxygen, which in turn increases her pain.

I look at the young mother lying on the bed with her eyes closed, resting peacefully with her baby girl beside her. Long and slow, I say to myself, that's the secret. I get into the Malagasy tempo and for the next few days I feel that even my heartbeat has slowed down. In this place time is not measured. Not during birth and not during life. Everything happens exactly as it should; there is no reason to hurry it along. Pitocin is given only to "help" the contractions become stronger, not to increase the tempo. The tranquility of the souls here is an expression of their belief that life is not controllable. We cannot control what happens, and certainly cannot control the forces of nature.

Dr. Christian Northrup, a holistic gynecologist, wrote in her book *Women's Bodies, Women's Wisdom* that a woman will give birth in the same way that she lives her life. It is no wonder then that the Malagasy women, who are used to hard physical labor, who accept life and death as normal and who accept struggle and pain without complaint, will be able to have a natural childbirth experience. Whereas in modern life, where pain is so feared that it must be defeated at all costs, women cannot have such an experience.

I part from these wonderful women with hugs and tears, even though nothing binds us except for the most primal experience that we shared. I part from the new baby I will never see again and from her young mother. I part from the grandmothers, the children, the goats and chickens in the yard. I leave this small island and say thank you to the palm trees that fan out like peacock tails against the sky. They are called travelers palms, because among the folds of their gigantic leaves water gathers, to be used by weary travelers in need.

Arriving on the big island of Madagascar I begin the search for more midwives. Tio, one of the Keepers of the Rainforest who speaks English, tells me of his Aunt Rina Zaza Ravobert. Tio suggests that we go to her village and meet her. It is possible to get to the village by car but will be difficult, so it's better to go by way of the forest. Tio guides me and a group of people who have joined us, through the forest. He knows every tree and branch. He is sure-footed and silent as he leads us calmly through the tangled forest. Everything is very green and lush and the gurgle of water can be heard in the distance. Here and there a patch of sky can be seen through the tops of the huge trees. Luckily it is not pouring down rain today, as it usually does.

Suddenly Tio stops and we all stop behind him. We are breathing heavily from the steep climb. He listens. I hear only the wind in the branches, the breath of the forest, the whistles and chirps of birds. Tio lets out a long whistle that rises and falls, and from somewhere on the other side of the valley an answer comes. He asks something with another long whistle and the answer is not long in returning. A slow symphony is being gently and lovingly played between a man and a bird.

We continue to walk, and as I walk along by his side, I listen. After a while the cells of my body seem to be attached to the leaves, to the sky, to the earth, and to the sounds. I feel as if a part of the wind and the boundary between myself and the universe has dissolved. All is in perfect harmony and the forest is in my eyes, skin, stomach, knees, hands, and I am in every part of the forest.

We walk for many hours in the rustling woods.

Tio explains to me that Madagascar has different types of taboos, and the events of a day are influenced by positive or negative forces. If the taboos are ignored, the result can be very destructive. The powers of the ancestors influence what happens, and they will decide what punishment will descend on whoever has broken the law.

When I point to a bush and ask its name, Tio tells me that one is not allowed to point with a straight finger at anything. That is one of the strongest taboos and is just not done. "Point with a bent finger," he says, "or you can use your whole arm in the direction you want to point to." He says that the absolutely worst thing of all is to point with a straight finger at someone's grave.

When we come out of the forest we can see the houses of the village in the distance. They are made of the local red bricks with few windows and pointed roofs. I can feel every muscle in my body, my shoes are covered in mud and my behind hurts from the many times I have slipped and fallen on the trail.

The fertile valley is spread out before our eyes in all its colors. Light brown and grayish with green and yellow. Some rice terraces are flooded in preparation for the rice planting and some are already filled with new bright green shoots. Lotus flowers and leaves float and cover almost the entire marsh.

I hear laughing voices and shouts of joy from a bunch of young men who are jumping around in the shallow water-filled ruts alongside the road. One of them calls out to the others and they all put their arms into the muddy water and pull out carp fish!

"Hey, I want to fish too," I say. In Israel, today is New Year's Eve, a holiday where we eat carp, so what could be better than to catch my own? I take off my shoes and remain in my short dress with my trusty walking stick. I place one foot carefully into the dark water and then the other. My feet sink into the mud and I fling my arms out to the sides trying to find my balance. The slippery mud slithers between my toes.

The warm water envelops my legs up to my thighs. The group of young men stares at me in surprise, but they can see that I am determined, so they begin to explain to me in French and sign language how to catch carp in a ditch with your bare hands. The method is to shout, clap your hands and stomp your feet in the mud until the frightened fish hide in the vegetation along the sides of the ditch. The fishermen then close in and feel around among the branches and leaves under the water until they catch a fish.

The young men show me where to hunt and I try, but come up empty-handed. One of the guys gives me a huge smile as he bends down and under the water puts a slippery fish right into my hands. It tries to wriggle away but I pull it out of the water and with a cry of victory, and raise it high for all the excited crowd to see.

Everyone roars in appreciation to see a wobbly white woman wave a dripping carp over her head. My throat fills with emotion from this experience. The young man simply wanted to make me happy and give the crowd a good laugh. He did not think, he just acted. That has been my experience of Madagascan society. People live together, work together, help each other to have fun and to deliver babies, experience joy and hardship together and will lovingly accept a carp-waving stranger into their midst.

Rinanzaza Ravobert has been the head midwife of this region for many years. Her hands are veined and the joints are swollen. She sighs and suffers silently. Her hands hurt after so many years of work in the fields, work in the house, and working to bring babies into the world. She is tired and speaks very softly and slowly, and a bit reluctantly.

I thank her for allowing me this opportunity to visit her and for her willingness to impart some of her ancient wisdom. Franza, her daughter-in-law, is a plump and energetic woman who translates for us. As usual, the room is full of neighbors, family, children, chickens and ducks who have come to witness this "event" but they are quiet. Franza serves us a drink. I take a sip and my mouth fills with the taste of burnt sawdust boiled in water. I sip it slowly even though it is strange.

"This is our most important drink," the old woman tells me. "It is made from water poured over rice burnt in a pot." This drink has many healing properties, as does rice itself. It's antiseptic and heals and provides energy.

Before she tells me about pregnancy and birthing, Ravobert wants to speak about Death.

"When someone from the village dies," she says, "his body is placed in a sarcophagus decorated with coins. The sarcophagus is placed some distance from the house, in a protected area, for one year. When the year has passed, the bones of the deceased will be laid close to the house, under stones from the rice field of the deceased.

"A ceremony called *famadihana* is held when the bones are moved to the grave and is a mixture of Christian and Malagasy traditions. All the village gather together, and what is left of the body is dressed in white lace and paraded from the sarcophagus to the last resting place of the deceased. There are many participants. Everyone wears necklaces of flowers, music is played loudly through speakers and everyone becomes drunk on rum. At the climax of this ritual a bull is slaughtered. This is to celebrate the happiness of the deceased, who is once again reunited with his family – both living and dead members.

"Father, mother, brothers, relatives, neighbors and acquaintances do not disappear when they die. They continue to give advice, to guide us, and to help those who remain alive. It is very important that everyone who is in any way related to the family stays in the family." R.R. sums up with this statement and all the people in the room nod in agreement.

"That is why we bury the placenta at the doorway to the house," she continues. "The placenta is a part of the baby. It is holy, like all other parts of the human body that live and breathe, and it is also part of the ones who no longer breathe. That is why it must be treated with respect and buried. Every time someone passes over the doorway he connects with the sacred body part that belonged to the mother and also to the baby. Through this body part the baby received everything he needed to grow, so that it is very important." Her grave expression stresses the seriousness of this fact.

"If a baby dies at birth we will not bury him. He will be called *zazaran* – 'water baby.' *Zaza* is baby and *ran* is water. We will float him down the river. He already knew the water of the womb and will continue to live in a place he is familiar with."

At this point I ask the question I always ask midwives: "What do you do if something goes wrong at the birth or if there is a complication you do not know how to handle?"

She answers very simply, "I ask my mother. I receive all my wisdom from my mother."

"Where does she live?" I ask.

"She died a long time ago," she answers.

"If someone has lived among us and then dies," she continues, "we must bury him. We will do everything we can to bring a son of the village to be buried here, otherwise his spirit will be angry and float around. This is the most dangerous situation, when someone does not have a proper resting place. A few years ago my brother's son disappeared as if the earth had swallowed him up. It was as though he had never existed. We frightened villagers sought for advice. We called a meeting of all the old women and the chiefs of all the villages around. A ceremony was held to bring back the vanished boy, or at least bring back his body.

"The wise elders told the boy's family to bring the pot that they always use for cooking rice. They must place the pot in the water of the rice paddy so that it will sail through the water and find the missing boy. And no one is allowed to cry. A tear of sorrow or worry rolling down a cheek will weaken the power of the magic and the boy will not be found. We decided that if worst came to worst, and the boy was not found, we would send money along the river to pacify his spirit. Luckily, after some time the body of the boy turned up and at last we could bury him."

The last meetings I had with Malagasy midwives took place in an area called Ilakaka. It took me three days to travel there from Antaribo, the capital. The first midwife I met was Raza Rimalala Simon. R.R. Simon is as ancient as her name is long, and takes great pride in the fact that under her care no woman has ever died in childbirth and there were no *zazaran*. The doctors and nurses at the local clinic send her all the problematic cases that they encounter.

She sits under an acacia tree on a blanket as old as she, and on her lap her baby granddaughter is sleeping. She learned about birthing from her mother and began to assist her at age 13. She has given birth to 11 children of her own. I glimpse a tear in her eye when she speaks about the continuation of the midwife dynasty. "One of my daughters is afraid of delivering and another is not good enough."

These painful words come to me through a translator. "There will be no continuation of this glorious lineage."

"Besides," she adds, "today all the young women go to the medical center for delivery."

According to the tradition that R.R. Simon inherited, preparation for birth begins at the start of pregnancy. For eight months, the mother-to-be needs to shower in warm water to open her womb, for example. I imagine that this is no easy task here where water must be drawn from a well. Simon says it is very important that the mother arrives at the delivery in good health, so that the birth will run smoothly.

"By the eighth month I already know the sex of the fetus. If the back of the baby faces to the left of the womb it's a boy, if to the right, it's a girl. I check to see if the baby turns over. If the head is still up, I massage the mother's stomach until the baby turns around. When the time draws near and the baby seems too fat, I give the mother *tamataba* tea to drink, so that the baby will be the right size and the birth will go well. If the tea does not work and the contractions don't become stronger this is a sign that it is not yet time, but if she is ready it will help the birth," she explains.

"What happens if the birth is taking too long or there is a complication?" I wonder.

"I will confer with my ancestors and if necessary I will send her to the medical center to get help," she answers, "but usually I can solve the problems. Even the doctors are amazed," she adds and straightens up with pride.

After the birth, the families put money in an envelope, place it in a hat and give it to the midwife to thank her. This bonus is called *ropcha* and guarantees that the breasts of the new mother will be full of milk, and also blesses the life of the midwife.

The baby in R.R. Simon's lap begins to move and awaken. She lifts up her head and gives a cry. Without hesitation R.R. Simon takes out her shrunken breast and gives it to the baby. The baby relaxes and now peeps from the old grandmother's lap with the nipple in her mouth. She looks around curiously to see what's going on. It's hard to tell if she is drinking or if the nipple serves as a pacifier.

On the tree we are sitting under there are children of all ages. The village women sit alongside us and on a log nearby are some youngsters who have come to see the white guest. Everyone listens with wide open eyes and mouths that suck on the lollipops I gave out when I arrived.

The women show me how they support a woman when she has her contractions. One pretends she is the woman in labor (she is in fact pregnant). She walks around supported on either side by her friends. I groan to signal that the woman is experiencing a contraction. "Ay ay," I moan and they all burst out laughing. I do not give up. I want to understand how supporting the woman on either side helps her to deal with the pains.

"This is what we learned, this is the proper way," they say. "And it is also important that the woman in labor be in the sun and drinks hot tea." Again, the warming element pops up. I ask if the woman in labor screams, and from the looks on their faces I realize that they do not know what I mean. So I show them. I lean forward putting one hand on my belly and one on my back and groan, emitting sounds of suffering. They laugh even harder and imitate me, thinking this is a game.

Then they go into a squatting position to show me how the baby comes out. They realize that I am referring to the stage of labor when the baby emerges, the stage of the pushing contractions, but not one of them gives a groan or any sign of pain.

I try once more to ask about pain and "Birth hurts" is the answer, as so many other midwives have answered me before. R.R. Simon says this very casually as she continues to chat with the women around her, giving it no importance whatsoever. There is no need to discuss it further. It is simply a fact, like the sun shining.

The grandbaby of the aged midwife continues to nurse peacefully from her shriveled breast while she tells me about the placenta. The *zandrazaza*. She pretty much repeats what R.R. (Tio's aunt) had told me. R.R. Simon also tells of the burial of the placenta as if it were a living body, and the tradition of burying it close to the doorway.

"After the *zandrazaza* comes out, I check it thoroughly to see if it's whole. When I am looking at it I sometimes see wings of a hawk or a dragonfly or of an eagle. This is what the soul of the newborn received at birth.

"What if the placenta is eaten by animals or insects?" I ask.

"That is very bad!" The audience seems frightened to even hear mention of such a dreadful idea.

The women serve us a platter of samosas filled with mincemeat. These are very fresh and tasty. I sit on the ground to eat with the old woman, the baby, and the flies that buzz around. The children have lost patience and have started jumping about.

In thanks, I place an envelope with the requested *ropche* in a hat that I borrowed for the occasion from my driver. I wish upon R.R. Simon and all her descendants long life, prosperity and goodness. Next, I go to the medical center to speak with the nurse. She is the only nurse they have and is responsible for the treatment of snake bites, high fevers, and birth defects. She has harsh criticism of traditional midwifery.

"Drinking *tamamaba*," she explains with a note of annoyance, "is dangerous and can even cause abortion of the fetus. All our efforts to convince the young pregnant women and midwives to use this with caution, do not help." But even here in the medical center the old ways are respected. "We separate the placenta immediately after delivery and give it to the family," " the nurse tells me. "The *nipoche* (umbilical cord) is dried out and given by the family to the *zebu* bulls to eat.

After the birth, the porridge prepared for the mother contains a special type of tiny shrimp called *patza*. This porridge will ensure that the mother's breasts have a lot of milk.

Not far from the clinic I meet with another elderly midwife, R. Razananzeva. She smiles a toothless smile at me while she prepares cream for baby massage. She brings water from the well and specific plants that she picks at dawn from the marshland. Right now she is pounding them and she shows me the plants, names them, and tells me their healing properties.

The *chimativnia* leaves will unite the baby with his soul, so that his life will be long and good. Another plant solves serious problems that even hospitals cannot cure. I do not understand what these problems are, and she doesn't understand what I don't understand, so she smiles and we leave it at that. The plant that connects the baby to his ancestors is called *anamelondrazna*. It resembles ginger in form and taste.

She grinds together these three plants with the well water. She says that the water is sacred because it is continuously renewed, and explains that this mixture makes the baby healthy. She also adds some salt, which she says prevents disease. I will hear of the antiseptic quality of salt again when I meet with Muslim and Druze midwives in Israel. While she grinds the plants she prays in Malagasy combined with French, to bless her actions. Her humming blends with the chanting coming from the church across the way.

A young daughter of R.R. arrives. Her chubby baby looks at Grandma warily. On the windowsill two gigantic ginger cats are sunning themselves.

"This baby was upside down in the stomach," says R.R. "It is possible to deliver a baby back side first but it is much more complicated, so I turned him over."

"How did you do that?" I ask.

She brings me to a mattress. I lie down and she removes my pants and exposes my plump stomach. She tells me that everyone is impressed by its whiteness. She places her hands on my stomach and shows me where the imaginary baby is. She pushes and I feel the spaces between my intestines move around.

"How did you learn to do this?"

"God gave me the knowledge," she explains.

The young mother undresses the baby. It is cold in the room and he starts to wail. R.R. calms him with soothing words. "It's good for you," she tells him, "you will be healthy and strong." She pours some of the holy water on his head and prays softly. She then spreads the cream she has prepared generously over his hands and arms, his feet and legs. She speaks to him and is also humming a melody to him. After she has massaged the arms and legs she crosses them back and forth. She then presses along the sides of his spinal column. She moves on to his cheeks, around his nose and his head.

When he is completely covered with green cream she holds him up by the ankles and turns him upside down. She then takes hold of just one leg and swings him from side to side. The baby lets out some loud cries of protest, but the young mother stands by watching, completely at ease.

R.R. continues to touch him and pray, and then catches his other foot and swings him again from side to side. She then places him on the table, wipes off the cream, smiles and kisses him and gives him back to his Mom. The mother wraps him in blankets, warming him up and calming him. She dresses him and puts him to her breast. He nurses eagerly and falls fast asleep.

The island of Madagascar is a very slow, patient, soft and flowing land and my stay here has made me more aware of physical sensations. In Madagascar I learned about the essence of pain. I saw the women working hard in the fields. Plowing, planting, carrying loads, washing clothes, and exposed to all the elements. I learned from them that hard physical labor and changes of weather are simply a part of life.

The conditions I lived in there were not easy for me. In all my travels, I sleep in the homes of the women I meet and endure the same extremes of heat and cold that they do. I march for hours to get from place to place as they do and get stung and sore as they do.

The difference is that the women of Madagascar do not place importance on any of these things. They work long and hard in order to be able to bring a morsel of food home. They stand in water for hours throwing nets to catch fish. They squat for months in the fields and carry heavy loads on their heads and children on their backs. They smell and see their menstrual blood, and their sweat pours down without ceasing. Water is not readily available all the time and it would not occur to them to mask the odors of their bodies. They live constantly and fully within their bodies.

The range of physical sensations that they go through is very wide, and includes pain on a daily basis along with many other types of physical and emotional feelings. The pain they feel in childbirth is nothing surprising for these women. They are well acquainted with extremes of bodily sensations, and the pain of childbirth is not even high on the pain scale for them.

It is very different for us Westerners, who have more or less deleted all physical sensations from our daily lives. We sit around a lot, move little, don't need to walk to get anywhere, take a lot of showers, use tampons so we will never need to have contact with our menstrual blood, and hide any indiscretions of our bodies.

We have little experience of and therefore do not trust in our ability to withstand physical hardship. This state of affairs brings us to the delivery in enormous fear of the physical process. The rumors we have heard about the terrible pains of childbirth, the notion that we are going to meet with sensations unknown to us, is all very scary. Even women who are well prepared in advance for this big physical strain are taken by surprise when it arrives. We do not know how to behave in situations where pain is involved, and so we want to give birth enveloped in the cocoon of the medical system. This seems logical to the medical professionals, who consider pain to be completely unnecessary to the birth process. According to this view, we might as well do without it.

We must learn and understand the importance of pain during the birth process, and understand that it has meaning and is vital to the correct functioning of labor. Women should be encouraged to cope with birth by using their innate resources and responses. There are many ways in which our society could promote this learning.

We could create a meaningful dialogue about pain.

We could analyze our fears about pain.

We could assess the different ways of lessening the power of pain over us.

We could come to understand that pain plays an important and positive role in the birth process.

We could understand what lies behind the gap between the worldview that sees pain as dangerous and as something to be eliminated at all costs, and   the worldview that sees pain as a positive and guiding element.

We could involve medical staff in helping the woman in labor who is ready and willing to deal naturally with the pains of childbirth.

During a pregnancy, I suggest to the woman that she surround herself with people who believe in her ability to give birth naturally, and who have the skills to help her to do so. I tell her to listen to birth accounts, which will give her first-hand knowledge of birth as an empowering experience. But trying to actively practice in order to be ready for the emotionally exciting and extreme physical sensations of childbirth cannot really prepare us to cope with the unexpected force of the experience.

In our Western world we understand things better by using our intellect and carrying out research, and these methods can definitely help us to cope with the pain on different levels. On the physiological level we can analyze – what is pain, what is the pain of childbirth, and why does it occur?

The International Association for the Study of Pain (IASP) defines pain as "an unpleasant sensory and emotional experience associated with actual or potential tissue damage ... These unpleasant sensations can also arise when there is no evident physical damage) or described as such."

Usually pain will arouse a reflexive action that distances us from the source of the pain, or forces us to recognize that something is amiss and we need to take action to fix the problem. As humans we react to pain not only physically, but involve our emotional and mental resources as well.

In general, pain is supposed to warn us that something is off balance and tell us to pay attention to it. Once the warning bell has sounded, the diagnostic phase sets in. For example, my head hurts, so perhaps I need to drink water or maybe I'm getting a migraine or my blood pressure is too high. After this phase we decide what to do. Drink water, take medication, sleep, or whatever.

Pain during childbirth is a signal letting us know that something out of the ordinary is happening within our bodies. The hormonal system is secreting various chemicals and our bones and ligaments are moving. Everything is in a state of change to allow the baby to come out. This warning is beneficial, and tells us that the final process is about to begin and that soon the baby will be born. Our psychological and emotional perception is on another level. That is, our awareness of the essence of the pain and its importance in childbirth.

Our warning mechanism to pain works in a very unique way during childbirth. It is not warning us of danger, but is alerting us to the fact that this natural and healthy process is occurring. Pain during childbirth has three sources:

1. Pain from contractions.

At the time of labor the functions of the brain move to the limbic (survival mode) area of the brain. Oxytocin is secreted into the blood system from the hypothalamus glands, whose job is to create contractions and also to enhance the process of bonding between mother and baby. The pain felt during contractions is from the uterus. The muscles contract for 20-80 seconds, and then there is a break when the uterus rests until the next contraction. The contractions will cause the entire cervical canal to open up enough for the baby to pass through. Along with oxytocin, other pain-relieving hormones are released.

2. Pain that stems from the stretching of the ligaments.

In order for the baby to be able to pass through the pelvis, hormones are secreted which soften the joints and the ligaments of the pelvis so that it can expand sufficiently.

3. Pain caused by the friction between the baby's bones and the bones of the mother.

The baby's skull rubs against the pelvic bones of the mother and this causes pain.

When we understand how pain is effective in causing the labor to progress, and guides the woman to move her body into the best possible positions for helping the baby to insert himself into the pelvic area, it becomes possible for us to treat the pains as friendly and helpful, which will greatly increase our ability to handle them.

Every person has their own personal neurological stamp, which determines how she interprets pain. This imprint is formed by genetics and by the constant sensory experiences that she goes through during her life. That is to say, there is a physical foundation for pain, but it is highly influenced by personal and cultural factors.

Pregnancy and childbirth are a golden opportunity for a woman to learn about her body and sensory perceptions on a deeper level than she is used to. She can learn to listen to body signals, understand what they are telling her, and gauge her responses.

In order to improve the ability to cope with pain, it is advisable to prepare one's body physically. Every midwife whom I ever spoke to during my travels emphasized the importance of preparing the body and taking care of one's health as factors which increase the chances of a good and safe delivery.

Exercise such as swimming, walking, and dancing all make the body stronger and better able to cope with the powerful sensations a woman will encounter during the birth. Yoga and martial arts are also helpful techniques for learning to listen to one's body and connecting to a wide range of sensory experiences, as well as strengthening the muscles.

There are many methods you can use to prepare your body. Some make it stronger and more flexible. Some also teach you to listen to the clear messages your body sends out. In yoga and other forms of exercise you also learn to breathe, to look within, and to relax.

These methods may also teach you to look at life events as an on-going learning experience. Consistent focused exercise of this sort will teach you to examine your physical and emotional reactions to things that happen to you both inside and out.

In yoga, the body acts as a laboratory in which we test our development and ability to handle situations. The yoga positions make us stronger and more flexible, and at the same time provide us with stamina and spiritual fortitude. All of this can help us to be better able to listen to our bodies and to handle the pain and emotions during labor. It is also worthwhile to decide beforehand which natural systems of pain management you wish to use. You can choose between massage, water birth, breathing, movement, or a combination that most suits you.

One of the ways in which I assist a woman in labor to overcome her pain is to remind her that the pain is only temporary and will soon pass. When a woman asks, "How long will it hurt like this?" and gets the answer, "We cannot know," it is hard for her to believe that it will ever be over. She quickly abandons all previous intention of withstanding the pain.

In order to help her, I break up the time into manageable pieces. For example, the time it takes for one contraction to pass is six or seven breaths. Knowing that the contraction has a beginning, middle and end makes it easier for her to endure it. At the births I accompany I ask the birthing mother if she can manage another 10 contractions, and usually she answers yes. The average duration of 10 contractions is 40 minutes, and within that time many things can occur. Even if the progress according to the outside measurement of dilation does not increase, every contraction still means some progress of the baby into the pelvis.

When 10 contractions have passed, I tell her that we will see what to do.

I remind her how important the pain is. That it is guiding her in the deepest dance of her life to change position, that the pains are teaching us how to make way for the baby. This encourages her to continue. I tell her that she is doing wonderfully and that each contraction leads her closer to the actual birth. Even though the numbers might not show it, the birth canal is opening.

Many pregnant women who prepare themselves physically to be able to go through labor naturally are still taken by surprise at the moment of truth, and ask for pain relief. Afterwards they often express regret that they "broke down" and did not "do it right." This makes me wonder, and raises some questions about how this grading system of birthing came about.

How did one way become "better" than another? Why can't we be more understanding and forgiving of ourselves?

Why do we measure ourselves by some standard without a deep look at our own individual way of being? Where is 'the woman who "just knows" and where did she disappear to? Can we be flexible and love ourselves enough to be aware of our own changing needs?

I believe that during pregnancy a woman should focus deeply on her physical, mental, and spiritual state. She should organize her delivery room rite of passage as a meaningful life event (at least as important as the wedding), and have honest and direct communication about her needs with the people who will be around her during pregnancy and present at the delivery.

A woman who does these things will be less critical of herself and able to accept with love and happiness whatever situation unfolds at the time of the birth, even if she changes her plan. She will handle whatever happens during the delivery in her own special way, because she knows she has done all that she can.

A woman who has prepared herself to deal with extreme pain and during the birth changes her mind, will still be able to accept her decision with joy and without feelings of failure if she knows she has done all that she can. She will know that the change from her original plan was right for her and her baby. The use of pain relief for a birthing mother who has done her very best can still allow her to be inside the process, to let go completely, and the birth will progress well.

One of the basic things to know about planning for labor is that it is only a plan. It is infinitely valuable that during the real action the mother must be flexible and relaxed and willing to accept whatever comes. A birthing mother who has done the best preparation she could, and comes up to her pain boundary and changes her plan, will still give birth in a flexible way, suitable for her and her baby's needs.

Sticking to a plan can stick the birth process. Using technology during delivery is one of our available options. An empowering experience is one in which the birthing mother knows that she has done her best for herself and her baby. If the need for medical intervention arises, and we can respond and listen to it with acceptance and joy, the birth will be good for both mother and baby.

The knowledge that birth can occur in a trance state and that it is normal to lose control and let go of "normal" behavior even when using technical measures, will still allow the experience to take place on a very high spiritual plane.

A Moroccan midwife whom I met in Israel spoke to me about birth pain in much the same way as midwives around the world do. "But of course birth is painful, very painful. If it didn't hurt, how would the woman know to appreciate what has been given to her?"

Every birth is a cosmic occurrence. No two births are alike and never will be. The appearance of a new soul on earth needs to happen amid fanfare, accompanied by drums and cymbals and a lot of drama.

Tamatava. Traditional medicine in Madgascar

Smiling girls on the road

Rinanana Janet

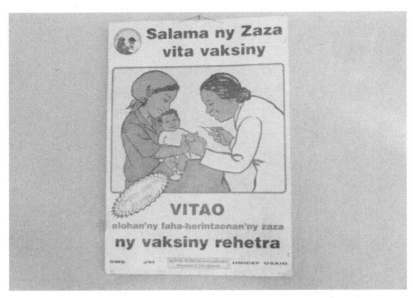

Health recommendations on Isle San Mary Madagscar

Fishing in the mud

The Gambia - The Fear

The odor hits me with a hammer. It is the smell of birth, mixed with the smell of feces. Every birth has a similar smell. The smell of secretions from the vagina, from the anus, from the mouth and from the skin pores.

Elizabeth is sighing and moaning on the bed. She is a very large woman with very dark skin, as only a West African can be. She is about to give birth in a hospital in Banjul – the capital of The Gambia.

On the wall are posters about easing the birth process for the mother in labor. One shows a white woman on a physio ball. Another shows a birthing pool, a shower stall. One lists instructions in case of emergency. All of these are in English.

The windows are broken and dirty. The walls are stained with older and newer blood. The bed is rusty, with a vinyl-covered mattress. The sink contains dirty pans from a previous birth. Only the curtains are cheerful and pretty with colored flowers. The heat is immense. Steamy and hot. Sweat trickles under my dress until it surrounds my buttocks. I am completely drenched; even my eyebrows sweat.

After a while I locate the source of the stench. It is coming from a small pile of feces in a corner. Nausea rises in my throat along with anger.

I came to The Gambia to meet Shelli, an Israeli friend who had told me about a method of massage done on very young babies here. She is the head of a humanitarian organization whose purpose is to broaden educational opportunities. She identifies locals who are literate in English and equips them to teach one other person who cannot read or write. Shelli invited me to stay in the compound of her organization in Serrekunda, a large town on the outskirts of Banjul.

The compound where Elizabeth, a birth mother, lives contains rooms and houses, all attached to each other and all surrounding an open yard. It is enclosed by a wall made of bricks and planks. Inside the compound live women who are in some way related, and their children.

They very happily accepted me and I immediately became a part of this small tribe of older and younger women and their offspring, plus a few young men who seemed to do nothing much during the day. When the women heard that my profession is pregnancy and birthing, they asked if I could do anything to speed up Elizabeth's labor.

"Why speed it up?" I asked.

"Because it is late," they answered simply.

As I am a foreigner, I decided to wait and see what would happen, and I politely declined. In the evening Elizabeth said that she felt something beginning to happen. By the next afternoon it was clear that she was having contractions and was ready to give birth.

I asked if I could accompany her and was given a definite yes. On the way to the hospital Elizabeth gripped the handle of the taxi door until her long black knuckles whitened. Her breath came slowly and with great concentration. That was the only evidence that she was having contractions and that they were painful. With us in the taxi is Janet, who is a traditional midwife. She is elderly and always smiling. Her head is wrapped in the local fashion with a colorful scarf made of the same material and pattern as her dress.

The hospital is situated in the heart of the capital city. It is an impressive building that has seen better days. Janet refused to go with us into the delivery room. "I don't like doctors," was her modest excuse. In fact, for years now, the practice of traditional midwives had been banned from all government hospitals. On the other hand, I was allowed in without a single question.

So here I now am with Elizabeth in the delivery room.

The nurse questions Elizabeth and I learn that this is her ninth birth. One of her babies had died after birth (no mention of how), leaving her with seven children. She was not asked about the father. In The Gambia it is common that the father is not around or is perhaps unknown. The children are solely the mother's responsibility and most likely not all from the same father. After these questions Elizabeth was invited to lie on the stained mattress.

Now Elizabeth and I are alone, surrounded by the curtain. Old and dirty medical equipment is scattered around. Elizabeth pees into a colored plastic bucket provided for this purpose. Then she lies down on her side, dripping with sweat and moaning.

I ask for some water for her, but am told apologetically that there has been no running water in the hospital for three days. Also, no electricity. On a spur of the moment decision I whisper to Elizabeth, "Dear, I will go to bring water, I will be back shortly." She nods her head tearfully and looks deep into my eyes, breathing heavily.

Outside, hundreds of people sit or stand on the dirt road surrounding the building, waiting. They wait very patiently, accepting whatever fate may bring. I cross the path to the colorful shops. One sells used clothing laid out on a shaky table. Another stall is just a pile of tomatoes on a cloth on the ground. For a few cents, one woman sells homemade coconut cookies from an aluminum pot on her head. I buy two plastic fans with colorful peacock and flower designs and two big bottles of water.

I run back, short of breath and ask, 'How are you?" Elizabeth only groans and mumbles something without opening her eyes. On the other side of the curtain can be heard the groans of other women in labor and the cries of a newborn baby who has just come into this world.

I see a nurse and ask her if someone can come and clean here. "Soon someone will come," she replies impatiently, and sure enough a cleaner in a blue uniform does appear to be coming towards us. She drags her feet along with a bucket of murky water. She looks exhausted as she empties the water onto the floor and with the mop now spreads the feces to cover the entire floor so that not one inch remains clean.

"It's not clean," I tell her.

She gives me a stony glare and swishes the mop around some more. "Now is good?" she asks. I try to smile and ask, "Maybe a bit more?"

Elizabeth has been hooked up to an intravenous drip while I went out for the water.

"What's in this?" I ask the nurse.

"Pitocin," she answers

"Why does she need Pitocin?"

The nurse raises her black eyes to me, thinks for a minute and then says, "Because the birth is taking a long time."

We had arrived there only an hour before, so I did not understand how this could be considered long. Elizabeth was already fully dilated and I wonder why they were giving her a catalyst. There was no reason to interfere with the birth process. The attitude here is clearly that the hospital decides for the patient and that the people have no voice in the matter, even in childbirth.

Perhaps my presence that influenced the 'field.' British colonization has left a profound mark on The Gambia and I, a white woman who in their eyes has importance and money, am a representative of that modern, rich man's world. Perhaps the hospital and its staff are trying to impress me by using the drip, so that I will consider them up to date and modern.

Elizabeth's water breaks.

Because there is a lot of AIDs in Africa and I ask the nurse for gloves. She looks at me unhappily and leads me to the end of the hallway. A large wooden closet stands there, carved and elegant (probably left by the British). She opens the doors and on the empty shelf sit two rubber gloves. I look at the nurse apologetically and take only one.

Elizabeth has begun to push. She emits low throaty growls like those of a wounded animal. The nurse and I exchange looks; we understand the meaning of these sounds and go to Elizabeth without speaking. I stroke her, wetting her lips with the water, fanning her face with the colored fan. Elizabeth speaks only Mandinka, the language of her tribe, but she understands that I am trying to comfort her. The touch of my hand on her brow and the cool water on her lips tell her all. She is away from the women who usually surround her, she is in fear of the medical establishment and does not understand their language, but she knows that I am here for her.

A few more pushes and the baby is out. A chubby boy lies between her legs in a puddle of amniotic fluid and other liquids. He mews softly. Elizabeth signals for me to bring her bag and she takes from it some pieces of cloth. She gives one to the midwife, who wipes the baby, wraps him up and gives him to his mother.

Elizabeth looks him over with a tired eye. Worried, her look tells him the whole history of her roaming in this world, her poverty, her many children and few opportunities. It is the look of a woman who has seen much and cares little.

It is hard for me to witness this whole scenario. No electricity, no water, no family or friends around her, no sheet on the bed, no monitor, no sanitary pads, no soap, no money, no food. Dangers lurk everywhere. Not that the birth itself is dangerous, but the un-hygienic conditions that abide here in a city hospital with no proper medication or medical equipment. I am feeling very tense, upset and depleted and I leave Elizabeth in haste. On the dirt road it is now afternoon. The waiting line for a taxi is not as long, and I lean against the crumbling fence and vomit until I have nothing left.

In The Gambia, the chances of a woman coming through delivery completely well are not high and the chances for her offspring are even lower. Just to get through a normal day and feed your family you must wake up and create something out of nothing. There are not a lot of choices available.

I cry and cry about the fate of the women here, and finally wash my face with some bottled water and wander the streets with puffy eyes.

I arrive at Big Tree Junction. Named after a huge tree growing in the dusty road, that 40 men can join hands around. The call of the Muezzin is heard in the distance. The street comes to a halt, men and women heed the call to prayer and kneel down. I do not kneel, but I pray in my heart for the new soul born today into a puddle of filth.

Back in the compound a few hours later, the old midwife Janet and the rest of the women greet me and are pleased to hear that the birth went well. Shelli is also there and looks me in the eye and says quietly, "Welcome to The Gambia." She hugs me and adds that she notices that some of the gleam has gone from my eyes.

I go to the market with Mago, a very pretty younger woman. Two of her sweet daughters come along. They sing Frère Jacques in French, even though their mother tongue is Mandinka and their second language English. Mago is once again pregnant. Her Senegalese husband is married to a white woman in Sweden, but comes to visit Mago every year and makes her another baby.

She buys four tomatoes, one and a half cups of rice and five huge okras. Half a cup of red palm oil in a plastic bag, a few pieces of cassava (yucca) and three slices of dried fish. We must also carry four sticks of wood, which will be turned into charcoal for cooking the lunch. The sun is scorching, so I buy her a small Coke along with some cigarettes and two bags of coffee, each containing a spoonful of Nescafe.

Once we are back at the compound the fire is lit, the pot is washed, the food is chopped and seasoned with salt and hot peppers. After two hours, all is ready and everyone is invited to come and eat. The young men of the compound, who have successfully passed another day of doing nothing much that I can see besides rolling and smoking joints and preparing and drinking *ataya* (a very powerful and sweet green tea), come along to eat with the women and children.

It is already long after noon and everyone is hungry. Each person touches the basin with their left thumb and eats only with their right hand. They nimbly scoop up rice and some sauce and roll this into a ball which they place in their mouth. I manage to somehow make a small ball and get it in my mouth. Fireworks go off in my head – it is spicy, extremely spicy. I look around in shame but apparently only I find it hot. I roll another ball in my clumsy way but some falls back in the bowl on the way to my mouth.

In the food bowl everyone carves out their own slice of territory while eating. While I dig into the rice I am creating walls with my neighbors. At some point the wall dividing my section and someone else's collapses onto my side of the pit. Apparently this signifies that today is my lucky day! A day in which my wishes may come true.

In tribal life, territory is very significant. Everyone is completely responsible for everyone else in the tribe. No one really owns property, but all are partners in all things both socially and physically. Here in this communal food basin a game is played with make-believe territory. So today is my lucky day, the wall fell into my section and everyone laughs together.

The following day the compound is buzzing. Everyone is busy cleaning and cooking and arranging. Elizabeth is back from Banjul and a new baby is here. Elizabeth lies in bed. She and the baby are taken care of, fed and fussed over. It is the natural thing to do. A woman after labor is taken care of by her friends.

I sit on the edge of the bed, looking and smiling at tiny Albert. Elizabeth looks at him with indifference. He gives out a small cry and she brings out a huge breast and feeds him while he lays at her side. When he is through, she gathers him up and offers him to me. I look at her, smiling, and take him onto my lap. "Take him. He is yours," she says.

I do not understand the words which are spoken in Mandinka, but Mago, who is cleaning near us with a rag, stops what she's doing and explains to me as if this was perfectly normal. "She says that you should take him with you to your country. You were at his birth and so he belongs to you, and with you he will have a better future."

I am taken aback. She is completely serious. She asks it of me again. In spite of the pleading and beseeching in her voice and eyes, I refuse. My friend Shelli takes me aside. "You are a *toubab*," she explains. "This means 'white' and for Gambians this means you are very rich and live in a paradise of plenty. They do not meet many whites here and whoever comes is either a tourist or someone from a charitable organization. Many white men come for cheap sex and women also come to find a lover and will pay for his services."

I tell her that the women in the compound ask for money all the time. They think I should buy them groceries, clothes, diapers, medicine, etc. "I don't mind paying for being a guest here and for what I learn from them," I say, "but at the same time it makes me feel uncomfortable that I am being taken advantage of and treated as 'other' than them."

Shelli smiles and says, "Yes, some of that is a guilty conscience. We Westerners unconsciously feel we must recompense for the immensely long period of imperialism, colonialism, and slavery that Western countries imposed on Africa. That we can somehow make up for the devastation of human and natural resources."

"But there is something else at play here," Shelli adds more gravely. "In Gambia the highest moral value is to give to others. Mutual aid is a fundamental virtue that allows life to have some semblance of normalcy, even though the people live under a corrupt dictatorship that provides little or no stability or infrastructure.

Very difficult living conditions and extreme poverty along with fear of the evil eye all play a role in how life is constructed, but he who has *must* give to others. This is a basic and intrinsic value. In return, you earn status 'points' with the community and family, and also with the spirit world. Generosity means security in the face of all kinds of problems.

The next day when I am at the market, I look around me with changed eyes. The stalls are full of life, color and movement. The small cloths spread on the ground hold piles of tomatoes, peppers and green leaves brought by women from their gardens. They hope to earn enough at the end of the day to be able to buy a cup of rice or some fish for dinner.

The women wear beautiful colored garments with matching head scarves. Their babies are tied to their backs and other toddlers sit by their sides. Men and women walk by carrying heavy loads on their heads and there are many cripples. Some lucky ones have a battered wheelchair, while others crawl on the earth.

A tall, striking woman stands with her coconut/peanut cookies. I ask for one to taste. The inflated *toubab* price is one half of a dalasi (around two cents). When she receives this sum from me she goes over to a cripple and gives it to him. I will see this over and over again during my trip.

Communal life in a place where physical life is so hard demands a very clear behavioral code to provide for mutual support. The belief in miraculous powers, devils, spirits, and a higher power can go a long way toward encouraging good behavior. It also adds another dimension to life, making the mundane more interesting. A person who does not behave according to the social rules will get his just desserts.

Back in the compound the beautiful Mago takes care of Elizabeth's baby. Mago is tired and her daughters are also in the room. The small room is full to bursting with the enormous Elizabeth lying on the bed, which is decorated with brightly colored ornaments. Janet is leaning on the doorpost and grinning, various visiting girlfriends are also present and of course the baby, also lying on the bed.

The washing of the baby is a serious undertaking and every

Gambian baby undergoes it daily. A bath and then a massage are given by an experienced woman or the midwife who helped to deliver him. Baby Albert is placed on Mago's legs. She wets him and soaps him with Dr. Fisher baby soap! A symbol of the relative wealth of this compound. After this, Mago rubs shea butter between her palms and spreads it all over the little body and begins the massage.

She goes over every disc of his back one by one, and using a deeper touch goes over his hands and feet. She gently works his knee and hip joints and then crosses his arms and legs. She presses particular points on his face – either side of his mouth and nose, his cheeks, and above his eyelids.

Afterwards she shows me how she releases pressure in his head that had built up during the birth. She does not explain why it is done, she does not know. She only says that this is what is done, it has always been done this way.

She clasps the little ankles and holds him upside down. After this, she waves him in the air holding his hands and then, to my great consternation, lifts him in the air by clasping his neck, with one hand on the nape and one on the chin. His hands are fluttering to his sides. Finally, he is put back on her knees and I can breathe again.

Mago smiles with her dark eyes flashing. Her perfect white teeth shine in her perfect black face and little Albert also seems perfectly happy. He and all the babies born in Gambia, Senegal, and the surrounding regions seem lucky to be given this regimen, which creates strong muscles, flexible bodies and straight spines, and releases tension.

The baby lies on the bed and Margo ties a lucky charm around his middle. Every child gets one to protect from the evil eye, diseases, and other childhood maladies. It is made of very thin leather strips with a tiny leather pocket attached containing a scroll with blessings written by the local marabout (witch doctor in French).

Shelli explains that most Gambians are animists who believe that everything has a soul, whether animal, plant or mineral. There are souls without bodies and various gods with human traits. The people hold ceremonies to ask the unseen forces for help in any new undertakings.

Today most Gambians are Muslims, but still respect the ancient powers of their ancestors and of nature. For example, they still speak of Mami Wata – the goddess of Water – and if someone is sick or injured they will go to a marabout to be healed in one way or another.

Shelli says that even all the white people living in The Gambia believe in magic, because there is no other rational explanation for the strange things that happen here. One of her friends, a university professor, was unable to split up from her boyfriend even though she wanted to very much. One day when he was out of town, she decided to clean and paint the house. When she lifted the mattress she found a strange bug-like wooden object right in the center. Once she got rid of that, she was able to also get rid of the guy.

In The Gambia when people talk about an accident that happened – a tree fell on someone, a car stopped working, a house was flooded, a snake bit a child, money was stolen, or a sickness befell a family member, these events are seen as a result of a magic spell. The belief that a spell can be put on an enemy to change the course of his life is deeply entrenched in daily life. It influences actions and takes up a lot of people's time, occupying their thoughts. Most people go to a marabout to place or remove a spell. He charges money for his services and can also heal illnesses and give advice.

Magic can be seen as the cause of many disastrous occurrences, but it also influences actions between people and the community for good. It acts as a balancing mechanism, which urges members of the tribe to act benevolently toward one another and will often encourage acts of charity within the community. Magic may also be called upon to resolve disputes between individuals. When someone feels that he is in danger or confused, his explanation is that a spell has been cast on him. In order to understand what he has done wrong and to whom, he will turn to a marabout, who will investigate within the community. If he does not find the perpetrator the shaman will use other means to remove the curse.

Despite Shelli's explanations I feel a deep shock, and fear wells up inside me from what I am confronting here in The Gambia. To me, it seems like desperation and hopelessness. These feelings of fear have been with me since the moment I set foot in this country.

The Gambia is a thin slice of land surrounded by Senegal to the north and south. It is only 30–50 kilometers wide and 450 kilometers long. It lies along both banks of the Gambia River, which spills into the Atlantic Ocean. My landing in this country took place during the precious light of a glorious sunset over the Atlantic that could be seen beyond the airport. The airport itself is an old building made of tin at the end of the runway. A long line of passenger snake their way to the entrance to this building and it is hot. Very, very hot.

Sweat drips from all of us. From the Gambians returning home dressed in European clothes. From shirts that are trying to stay starched and from colorful traditional attire with matching head scarves. From babies tied on backs with cloth and from children dressed up in their finest clothes. People touch me, brush against me, without even noticing. The distance of body language here is not the same as the one I am used to.

Porters dressed in khaki drag the bundles from the belly of the plane and place them on a conveyor belt that does not work.

Nothing in this terminal works. Not the gigantic ceiling fans, nor the ancient computers, nor the flush toilet. Nothing is taken care of and everything is falling apart. There is no electricity. People push and are pushed to reach their luggage. I am stepped on, trampled upon, and loud voices and shouts surround me.

Somehow, I arrive in the line at Border Control. After a few more long and sweaty minutes standing in line a young officer asks for my passport. He turns it over, flips through some pages and turns it over again and again. How long can it take to examine a passport?!

Perhaps he came to work with some personal problems that day, or someone annoyed him and how did life manage to land him in this powerful position. I still do not realize or fully internalize that this is a police state. I have no previous experience of this at all. I look at the officer in his ironed uniform, which still manages to have a stink of sweat. He hands me back my passport and says something I don't understand.

Across from me are two tall and impressive officers. They catch me under my arms. I am quiet because even though I am terrified, for some reason I feel that everything will be all right.

"Missing document!" one of them says to me.

I have no idea what this document could be, but because I am white, with money in my purse, and sure of my innocence and firm in my resolve to achieve my goal, I turn to the officer on my right and on my left and tell them in simple English that everything is okay and would they leave me alone. I explain that I was assured by the British Embassy in Tel Aviv that all my papers were in order, so please let me go.

I am longing with all my being to get past this obstacle and get out of this stinky and sweaty arrivals terminal, but the officers insist. The English they speak weaves in and out between Wolof or

Mandinka or some other languages they know. Out of the corner of my eye I catch responses of discomfort from those around me. Signs that something is not right. They try to warn me and I start to realize that I should be very worried.

From out of the blue another officer appears. There is shouting, hand waving and unclear words. I start to be afraid. An American from an Aid office sees my plight and explains that a year ago a bunch of Israeli musicians came without proper papers and since then all Israelis are treated as suspect. Waterfalls of sweat begin to cascade down my back, but then the officer puts a big stamp on my passport and lo and behold – Approved!!

I make my way out of there as quickly as I can. From the start, The Gambia received me with the smell of sweat, the threat of power, and general unpleasantness. Some days after Elizabeth's delivery I go on a trip to the beach, to rest and take a breather from the suffocating atmosphere of the compound.

I travel in a van that is supposed to hold 11 passengers but is actually carrying 20 people, a brown goat, some chickens, and of course numerous babies. In addition to all of us, there is a youngster whose job it is to open and close the back door at the many stops on the way. He also puts the seats up and down to allow passengers to enter or exit. He collects fares and gives change and helps people with their bundles. There is no seat for him, so he does all this while hanging half out the door and at the same time smoking and drinking a Cola.

Every five minutes we are stopped at a roadblock. The doors open, letting in a wave of heat and dust and of course a policeman. He gives orders in an official voice and everyone on the bus takes out their identity papers, and the official slowly looks over each of them. Again I can smell the odor of fear around me and feel it creep into my body through my skin pores. The hair on the back of my neck and arms stands on end. Everyone is afraid and so am I.

Another roadblock, another paper search, and again the fear, and then the return of the documents and a quiet sigh of relief passes through the bus. But at one point the tension does not subside; the search is taking a long time, minutes follow minutes, time stands still and we passengers hold our breath. Around us there is chaos, dogs bark, peddlers shout their wares, but inside the van there is complete silence and stillness.

Orders bark from the mouth of the officer, who has medals and badges of rank pinned to his uniform. No one moves. Then comes another shouted order, louder this time, and the shaky voice of the bus fare boy calls out something. With no choice, two people stand up slowly in the crowded van. They are completely bent over and the smell of fear is now more piquant. I can hear my heart beating and my breathing becomes ragged.

The two doomed passengers make their way over bodies to exit. In a low voice I ask my neighbor what is going on. "Ghana," she whispers with closed lips. I understand that refugees come to The Gambia from other African countries in the hope of being able to better their lives. They know that many tourists from Europe come here and hope to befriend one and manage to get to Europe, or at least to get some money.

This faint hope causes many people to leave their homes and families and set off to Gambia – The Smiling Coast. The immigration officials have caught these two infiltrators and the chances of them being jailed or deported are now high. The Gambia aims to get rid of foreigners as much as possible.

The pain of the situation actually hurts my body. Without thinking, I search in my purse and take out two 100 dalasi notes. This is a large sum by Gambian standards. When the first young man's leg is next to mine I take his hand and push the bills into it. The minibus is paralyzed. Until now, one dared to bat an eyelash, but now the freeze is total. The young man slides the money into his pocket and without looking at anyone, descends with a jump from the bus. The ticket boy closes the door, the driver starts the engine, and we are back on the road.

The woman sitting beside me places her sweaty hand into mine and gives it a warm squeeze. A rush of joy mixed with flight or fight adrenaline passes from her skin to mine. The silence on the bus is thick and deep. Once in a while someone sneaks a downward glance at me.

After a few days at the beach I begin my journey to Baboon Island, where I hope to learn more about the mysterious Gambian baby massage. The trip is long, lasting a few days. Anna Gaye accompanies me – my friend from the compound in Serrekenda. She sets out from Banjul to join me on the first leg of my journey. She will ride with me up the Gambia River and we will part when I sail to the island.

She takes care of me as if I am a queen. She carries my bag, washes my clothes, and makes sure that my part of the food bowl will be full with the choicest morsels. I no longer try to stop her. I know better by now.

The Gambia River flows from the heart of Africa and splits Gambia down the middle before emptying into the Atlantic Ocean. At the height of the rainy season green vegetation covers both banks and is impenetrable. Only two weeks after the rain has stopped, the burning heat begins to kill off the wild undergrowth. Animals start to come to the river to quench their thirst and the river itself changes direction. In the dry season, sea water will begin to flow into the river. Conditions here are harsh and nature can be extreme and very fierce.

Anna Gaye speaks three African languages: Mandinka, Wolof (spoken by the second largest tribe in Gambia and Senegal), and Susu (spoken by the Guineans in her dance troupe). She also speaks English very well, the official language of The Gambia. She was a professional dancer but is now getting older and her hands and feet are twisted. She keeps me company on my way to meet with the traditional midwives in the bush (countryside), where they still practice a special ceremony each morning, washing the new babies and massaging them according to the ancient ways passed down from generation to generation.

We begin our trip in another local vehicle full of people and their belongings. The road is in very bad condition. This year the rainy season brought especially heavy rains, and the road on the south side of the river is completely washed out and practically impossible to drive on. On the northern bank, where we are, it is not much better and a distance of 100 kilometers takes two whole days to negotiate. We arrive at Farafini, the largest village of this region. We are welcomed into the fairly well-to-do compound of the chief (*alkalo*). He is a very wide man who rides a shiny red motorbike in his starched uniform.

We stay to sleep in his compound, and I find myself lying in bed with Anna Gaye and another two women. On the floor are children of all ages sleeping on mattresses. It is very hot tonight. The room is closed and stuffy. All my requests to open a window are met with stern looks. It is not permitted to open windows at night for fear of flying witches and creeping things.

I am exhausted the next morning but we go for a walk towards the river anyway. Strolling through the forest we come upon a hut surrounded by a well-constructed fence. It is painted white and looks exceptionally tidy compared to the other run-down huts. The surrounding area is very clean and carefully raked. In the yard are two more huts and a brick building painted white and sky blue. It's flat roof has another thatched roof above it.

It looks very unusual and I ask Anna what it is.

She turns a little pale and says, "It's nothing, let's go."

"If you won't tell me I will go in and ask," I insist.

"No, no!" she shouts in a fearful tone. "A white devil who steals women lives here. He turns them into his sex slaves. If they are lucky, he only photographs them for disgusting movies that he sells in Europe. If they are not lucky, he butchers them and eats their flesh."

With firm steps I approach the gate, open it and ask in a loud voice, "Anybody home?"

Anna Gaye quakes by my side. For her, devils and spirits are very real and not to be provoked. The old man who comes out of the neat house is a devil in her eyes and proof of all her fears. I see only an old white man who states his name as Jeff. He politely invites us to come inside.

Jeff had served many years in the British Navy. When he retired he bought a yacht and began to travel. A few years ago he had come upon the Gambia River and fallen in love with the country. He bought a piece of land, set up house and raises chickens and roses in the surrounding area. He says he is happy, does not miss London nor the family he left there. He has a Gambian woman, young and beautiful, and he loves his new life.

Anna Gaye begins to relax a bit. We sit on the roof of his house as darkness falls around us. The roof is protected from rain by the thatch, and netting is stretched all around to keep out insects and reptiles. It begins to rain and the deafening noise drowns out the humming and chirping of the bush.

Jeff is aware that the inhabitants think of him as a wizard and explains that he understands this. "I am a completely foreign element, white, old, with strange rules of behavior. For the locals, everything belongs to everyone and they would come in and out of here freely at all times if I did not stop it. Since I insist on keeping my privacy they assume I must be hiding some dangerous secret. Therefore I am an evil spirit and bring misfortune upon them. On the other hand, because I have my naval pension, I am an asset to the village economy and so no one harms me. I suppose my bribing the *alkalo* also helped my case a bit."

The rain does not let up and despite Anna's vehement protests we stay to sleep at Jeff's house. Anna and I share a bed and mosquito net. The bed bites, and I itch all over. Anna sleeps restlessly, turning over and kicking all night long. She constantly wakes me to check that I am still alive and not chopped into bloody bits.

In the morning, Anna and I part company. She wants to return to her family and I realize that the visit at Jeff's was too much for her. I am not sorry. I too want my independence back and I continue on my way to Baboon Island.

In the afternoon, after many hours of traveling on terrible roads, I reach the river and get on a boat that will take me to the island. A muscly young man is steering the boat. He knows all the twists and turns of the river. It is quiet, only the ticking of the motor makes a sound. He navigates among the branches, trying not to get too close to the hippos who rise up out of the water.

It was explained to me that they can attack humans if they are protecting their young, but my boatman does not seem worried. He guides the boat peacefully, occasionally pointing out to me some movement among the trees on the island. Baboon families are leaping from branch to branch. We see a large father baboon and the smaller sized mother with a baby hanging on her back. Then another two of different sizes. This constitutes one family of the many that are taken care of by American volunteers and locals who have been enlisted to save the baboons of The Gambia.

My driver stops for a minute to show me a bird's nest hanging from a low branch. The beautifully fashioned nest is oval and made from twigs and straw. Inside lies an egg. A wave rocks our boat, we rock the nest and it comes loose. The egg crashes onto the floor of our little boat. We look at each other in shocked silence. At our feet lies a puddle of yellow with bits of shell. Like two partners in crime, we smile apologetically. Later on, when we have reached our sleeping place for the night in the center of the forest, the driver will come to me with a sheepish grin. It shows his brownish teeth and he points to a photo of a bird with a curved beak. This is the bird whose egg we ruined by mistake.

The village of Baboon Island lies one and a half hours inland from the shore. The sunny dirt road leading to it is flanked with huge baobab trees on either side. The baobabs are full of hundreds of hanging nests.

Finally I arrive and meet Tiri, a toothless midwife who has been expecting me. She sits in the yard of her hut on a low stool. Dogs surround a swarm of noisy flies and there are a few chickens and donkeys. Four young women sit alongside Tiri with their new babies.

"This baby is sick in his heart." Tiri points to the chest of the baby lying on her lap. I can see the tiny chest rising and falling with difficulty. When he breathes there is a rasping sound. She places her two soft hands on his chest. His mother watches.

"How do you know it's his heart?" I ask and wait for the translator to present my question and give me her answer.

"The doctor who comes every two weeks told me."

Tiri's legs stretch straight out in front of her, resting on an up-turned bucket. By her side is another bucket holding water for washing the baby. On the ground is a sponge woven from plastic strings, soap, and a cloth for wiping the little one. She washes him while humming a quiet tune. The other women chat. One is breast feeding, one giggles. They speak in Wolof.

The baby gives himself to the old woman's hands. When she is done washing him, Tiri dries him and begins the massage. She first spreads shea butter, going over every tiny part of him. Stroking, pressing, stretching and crossing and uncrossing his arms and legs. She spread his arms out wide to the sides and works down each side of the spine. She presses points on his face. He makes soft bleats but does not cry.

According to a survey done by the CIA, the mortality rate for Gambian babies is 62 out of every 1000 births. This baby is very sickly and chances are that in the West he would not have been born at all. The parents would have been advised to terminate the pregnancy. Being born in The Gambia in these conditions and far from any modern hospital gives him little chance of survival.

The midwife smiles and places her strong and knowing hands on him. Afterwards the young mother takes him, dresses him and nurses him. Unfazed, Tiri shows me her midwife kit. A metal box containing a notebook that lists all the babies she has delivered over all the years. In spite of efforts by the government to institutionalize deliveries into local medical centers, the distances are still too great for many to get to the nearest town.

The notebook is full of wrinkled and stained pages. There are charts with the name of mother, father, baby's sex, date of birth, and the result – live or dead. There is a column with OK if the birth was at home and successful, or H if mother or baby had to be taken to hospital.

Afterwards, Tiri sings me the melody she sings to the mother during her delivery. Gambian traditions are usually handed down through the generations orally, and often in song. They are full of lessons about life, tell of events that happened within the tribe and dramatic natural occurrences. While she sings, she gets up and stands behind me, placing her hands on my back. I can feel the warmth of her hands through my dress. I feel strength and comfort flowing from her hands. She seats me on the stool and sits behind me, continuing to touch me soothingly.

She presses deeply into the small of my back, which is weak from my long, hard journey. The places she touches begin to throb and respond to her penetrating energy. I start to breathe deeply. Drawing in the smell of the dust and the trees, the goats and the heat, the plants of the earth. With my eyes closed I surrender to her touch. Even though I am aware of the others looking at me, I am also aware of the waves of pleasure and relaxation that are coursing through me. I felt so tired after all the challenging days on the road, and suddenly stimuli begin to surge through all the cells of my body and I feel them exploding under her hands.

The women who were drawing water from the well or just passing by, women who were coming from or going to the fields for cassava or other vegetables, start to gather around us with their children. They have flies in the corners of their eyes or around their nostrils.

The old woman leaves my back and smiles into my eyes and asks me, "Was it good? Did you understand?"

I did understand. I understood the feeling of belonging to a community. I understood even through my itching and pain, and through a yearning that arose in me and through my brain, where all thoughts were erased by the heat of the sun and by the totality of existence.

More women arrive. They carry water on their heads in large dripping buckets. Each of them has a chain around her neck with a cellphone attached. It is one of the necessities of life here and enables contact with the rest of the world. Another instrument that promotes belonging and cooperation.

The dripping women laugh, put out a hand to pick up a crying child, wipe snot with their fingers, shoo away flies, feed a piece of bread into a child's mouth, scratch themselves, sit, sway and chat.

I notice that my translator drags his foot and is limping.

"What happened to your foot?" I ask.

"I was born like this," he replies.

I try to ask him a few questions about it and how he managed when he was a small child.

"I didn't have it when I was small," he now says. "It happened only a few months ago. A big branch fell on me from that tree you see there. Do you see a branch is missing? It fell on me and it hurts."

I remember that both Shelli and Anna warned me that in Gambia facts can be slippery, changeable. You cannot tell why or what is the truth in the stories. They had explained that a story might be to ward off evil, perhaps to confuse it, perhaps to elicit funds from you.

Tiri is about to massage another baby. She lays him on her legs, washes him with warm water from the bucket his mother has brought. She soaps him gently with the sponge made from plastic and dries him. When he is dry she rubs him with shea butter and begins the massage. She starts at his shoulder and moves down his arms. Her touch is slow and firm. The baby's hands receive their own special massage. Tiri rubs every joint on every finger. When she finishes doing this also to the legs, feet and toes, she crosses the arm and the opposing leg. She spreads his arms out wide to the side and pulls on both of his feet together.

She then turns him over on his stomach to work on his pack, pressing the indentations above the pelvic bones. She massages his buttocks and travels up on either side of the spine, disc by disc, until she reaches the neck. She turns him back over on to his back and presses the groin area to spread it open. She presses the testicles gently and then massages his stomach.

She presses her fingertips on his chin, cheeks, both sides of the nose, over his eyebrows and on his forehead. His scalp receives a deep circular massage. She then holds him up by the neck, under his chin and nape and waves him in the air. At every stage she shows me where it is good to press harder and where to press very carefully. The babies are completely comfortable in her hands and fall asleep afterwards into a deep slumber.

From her toolbox, which lies at her feet, she pulls out a scale with a piece of cloth attached. She lays one of the babies on the cloth and is proud to show me that he has gained weight nicely.

I gave him *jambkatau* she says. "It is a plant that we make into a potion to assist the mothers, It is good for pregnant women, kills parasites, and cleans the stomach around the baby. It makes women more comfortable, helps the delivery, reduces pain and frees the afterbirth if it does not come out easily. After the delivery I prepare a different potion using the same herb. This now helps the blood circulation and improves milk production."

She shows me the plant. It looks similar to an opiate plant that is used regularly in Thailand and Vietnam as an anesthetic in cases of physical injury and also during deliveries.

"What else do you give during delivery?" I ask.

"I boil cassava root. It is always good and fortifies the woman."

"What do you do with the placenta? When do you separate the baby from the afterbirth?"

"I wait. I do not immediately separate it. I wait. Sometimes the afterbirth comes out still attached to the baby, and sometimes I tie the cord off with a bit of clean string and cut with a razor blade. I bury the afterbirth next to the house along with the blade that cut the umbilical cord

The women begin to plan what to cook for our lunch. They tie the babies onto their backs and start to chase after a rooster they have picked out. The rooster tries to escape his fate but in the end is caught, his throat is slit, and the women clean and pluck him and cut him up. Now they must bring the wood and the cooker, light the fire and boil water. The outside kitchen is next to the straw hut. Smoke and soot envelop them. Their backs are bent low as their hands prepare the vegetables, as they have done so many times before. The vegetables they have grown and picked themselves.

Two women pound grain in a large wooden mortar. The rhythm is monotonous and I become hypnotized by the tempo, the movements of the women, the voices of the children, and the smell of the cooking.

At the far end of the compound a group of men are sitting around making *ataya* tea, preparing it in three stages. They add a piece of charcoal from our fire to theirs. They add tea leaves to the bubbling water and then sugar. The leader lights a rolled cigarette and the pungent smoke swirls around his head. The joint is passed from hand to hand, mouth to mouth. The man leading the tea ceremony lifts the small teapot from the fire to lower the boiling. It will be brought to a boil again and again. The tea is addictive. The men enjoy each other's company and are glad to be lazy together.

Night is falling. The birds still chirp, but in the mud huts women put down crumbling mattresses for the children to sleep on. They are tired from playing all day. I lie down next to one of the women. The smells of the cooking, the soot and fire, the goats and donkeys and dust all surround me and mingle with the sounds of breathing. I fall asleep, tired out from the events of the day, and sleep dreamlessly.

My journey back to Serrekunda takes several days and includes numerous transfers of vehicles, stops for eating at the small roadside food stands, and mechanical failures of the van.

On the night of my return, Shelli, Anna, Margo and some other women go across town to attend a dance organized by women and only for women. The women save up their pennies to be able to pay for the drummers and hold the party every few months.

Women of all ages are walking to and fro along the riverside. There is a lot of debris around and some rickety homes consisting of wooden planks or plywood sheets, metal corrugate and whatever else was available. One woman catches my eye because she shines in her flashy dress. Her dress and matching head tie are mustard yellow with splashes of red, green, black and purple.

The closer we get to the site of the party, I notice more and more women in dresses that are identically patterned, but sewn in different styles. Some are long and flowing, some hug the breasts and hips. Each woman has her own style and every single one is completely original. They stroll about in their gaudy beauty like flowers in the night. They sway their buttocks flirtatiously; they wiggle and roll their hips. Everyone is smiling, chatting, busy and excited about tonight.

Anna invites me to go with her into one of the raggedy houses. I have to bow my head to enter, and try not to step on any crawling babies. Inside the room, in front of a large, smoky mirror hanging on the mud wall, women are getting dressed.

The first layer of clothing is lacy satin underwear. These go over black buttocks that are firm or crinkled, mottled or smooth, as the case may be. Small or large, all the women wrap their bottoms in these tiny panties which have a diamond pattern. Some of the women are young with flat stomachs and beautiful behinds. Some have breasts just starting to bud. The very small girls wriggle in imitation of their elders. Garters enclose thighs, brassieres of all colors hug breasts of all sizes.

One woman ties a woven string around her waist, another helps her friend gather up huge soft breasts with nipples even darker than her black skin, another one parts her lips at the mirror to check the flash of her dazzling white teeth. Everyone helps everyone else, trying things on, arranging, pulling and stretching. Everything should be exactly in place, to the complete satisfaction of each one.

Over and on top of the sensuous under-attire will come the dress, which will accent curves and be worn just so. They continue on to make up their joyous faces. Earrings are inserted in earlobes, bangles clatter on wrists, their nails are already painted with shiny nail polish. Mention must be made of their hair. Some have hair piled up high on top, some braided fancily, some decorated with beads, flowers, head bands and ribbons.

Outside, the drums begin to beat and excited voices can be heard. The drummers are also dressed as for a show – covered with dreadlocks, hats, necklaces, and jangling jewelry. Their long thick fingers, black on the outside and pale on the inside, create sounds that explode from the drums, which also are decorated.

Darkness falls as more and more excited women fill the area. There are no men present or allowed, except for the tall drummers with the long fingers. Some singing begins along with the drumming. The women sway and move their feet in rhythm with the drums and emit throaty melodies. Mouths open wide and hips begin to move. Arms are raised and chests move to the increasing rhythm. The chests rise and fall as everyone breathes together.

The tempo picks up even more, and I can feel my own stomach respond to the music and movement. The trees around us also seem to move with us; there is no longer one woman and another, we are all one body. The music seems to enter every cell of my body and moves me beyond my control. I become wet from all that I am feeling and I blush into the black night.

One woman enters into the center of the raging circle. Her skin shines with glistening sweat and her movements change to movements of sexual intercourse. Her pelvis moves up and down, and side to side. The drums make a deafening noise and the circle teems with emotion. The dancer drops to all fours into the sand in a spasm of ecstasy and her buttocks rise and fall, her breathing is vocal. Her sisters come in closer, hands, feet, stomachs, necks and heads coming together as one, breathing in and out as one, sweating and moving uncontrollably.

The music is inside me as the orgasm overtakes me. Waves of pleasure roll from my womb throughout my entire body. Each of my cells is alive and pulsating with pleasure, as I move with this collective orgasm together with my sisters.

Another woman takes the central position in the circle and everyone is with her in her journey, which breaks the boundaries of self and other. The music is louder and the rhythm slows down. Thunderous yet calm, gentle, comforting, stroking and then getting faster again. This goes on for hours and hours. We are lost to our senses, lost in space and time. The gods of love and sensuality are with us. Tremblings of pleasure and pain, sorrow and joy, happiness and also deep despair.

On the plane going home to Israel I am very itchy, and as I scratch I feel uneasy about my extremes of experience in The Gambia.

I have a stop in Barcelona. The floor in the airport is shiny clean back marble. I feel completely worn out and step into the WC. I burst into tears upon seeing the shiny bright faucets and stroke the cold black marble countertops.

Two days after my homecoming I am called to accompany a delivery in a birthing room in central Israel. I thank every single midwife and doctor I meet with a lot of feeling. Near the water cooler I stand with tears in my eyes. The cabinet full of medicine, the closets full of clean, ironed linens, the water in the shower and the light in the rooms all fill me with boundless gratitude.

In The Gambia I was scared in a way that I've never been scared in my life. It was an experience of continuous terror. Everything was extreme – the heat, the smells, the colors. From the minute I landed, I realized I had no control over anything. There were no clear laws and I was at the whim and caprice of any government officer. The delivery at the hospital in Banjul only added to my despondency.

My Gambian friends lead a life of poverty and deep deprivation without proper sanitary conditions. They have to pull up water from a well, there is no electricity most of the time, and the weather is extremely hot and humid. The government abuses the people and men have power over the women.

Health services are almost non-existent, and women suffer from diseases and injuries without proper care. There is very little infrastructure, the roads are terrible, the sewers overflowing, and when it rains even a short walk to the nearest tiny market stall turns into an ordeal.

Along with these feelings of fear I also felt that I had no control over anything. I never knew what time the bus would depart, how long the journey would last and what would occur on the trip. This uncertainty made me even more frightened. This never-ending tension gave me pains all over my body. The entire time I was there I ached. I was bitten, bruised, and sweaty. I was afraid of this constant irritation due to the weather, the insect bites, and the uncomfortable conditions. I was afraid I would have an accident or contract a disease. I was afraid I would die there.

I wondered about this and tried to ask the Gambians whom I knew if they too were scared about these things. Are they able to accept their reality and simply come to terms with it? Are they even aware of these constant threats to their health and safety? Are they driven by fear to take action, or are they too busy just trying to survive day to day?

From what I heard, I understood that they also are frightened about things, but added to the fear is the feeling of helplessness in the face of economic hardship. They fear for the men in their lives and for the future of their children. It seemed to me that in Gambia there are three main sources of fear. Fear of pain, of being hurt, and of death. All of these are intensified during pregnancy and labor.

Along with feelings of expectancy and excitement pending the arrival of a new baby, there is also fear of the unexpected. Giving birth is a state in which you are not in control and have no way of knowing what might happen. You do not know when it will occur, how long it will take, how it will go, and what the result will be. Even though it is a natural and healthy condition, in 10% to 15% of births something can happen and a complication set in. This is how things always were and continue to be in all cultures.

Complications range from very minor to major, and the health of both mother and baby is dependent upon the sanitary conditions and medical options available at the place of birth.

The WHO examines by geographical distribution the mortality rates during delivery and immediately afterwards. In countries with lower technological development the mortality rate for mothers is 700 in every 100,000 births. In Gambia, the situation is particularly bad. Even in government-run delivery rooms which should be giving adequate medical care there is no medical equipment, no water or electricity for days on end. No linens, no methods for cleaning or caring for the baby, and the mortality rate is even higher.

Elizabeth's birthing experience in Banjul revealed to me the dangers that haunt my women friends in Gambia. They are continually in a state of life-threatening danger and even more so when giving birth. Elizabeth was worried about the health of her baby during pregnancy, and had no recourse in the face of decisions by the medical staff or the insanitary conditions in the hospital. Anna Gaye put it very well when she described the hospital as a slaughterhouse. She said everyone she knows, also knows of someone who died during childbirth or had a baby die in childbirth there.

All these stories seem distant to us in the Western world. We have well-equipped delivery rooms, modern instruments, and well-trained staff. We have excellent nutrition and sanitation. In Israel, our mortality rate for mothers is 1.5 per 100,000.

So why are Western women so scared of giving birth? How is it possible that in such safe conditions, many of the women I meet through my work are not only scared of the pain, but also of physical harm and death. Their fear stems from social conditioning. There exists a kind of social epidemic that promotes fear. Very often birth is described as a painful and difficult experience which damages one physically as well as psychologically. The whole language surrounding birth is full of words that inspire fear and helplessness.

In research with different groups on social media, women were asked to describe their birth experience. Seventy percent used the words, Hell, scared to death, horrible, I wanted to die. Very few expressions were positive. Birth horror stories are much more common than stories that are empowering. Women also often speak of physical and verbal abuse by staff.

Pregnant women to whom I speak often express fear of pathological or psychological injury. "I am afraid I will tear," "…that they will cut me," "I am afraid I will be forced to do things against my will," "I am worried the baby won't be okay," "I am afraid I won't love the baby (first-born), or that I won't love the second as much as the first," "I am afraid I won't have milk…," "…that I won't be a good mother," "…that I'll die in childbirth," and on and on.

During the transitional phase of birth, when the baby will come into the world very soon, I often hear expressions like, "I can't go on, help me, I'm going to die…"

The medical system does not try to reduce the fear. Instead, it is often the cause of it. The batteries of tests that women must go through certainly make it seem that many dangers are lurking.

The expected pain is another big driver of fear when delivery is getting close. Pain is a very individual thing, and despite all attempts to describe it objectively, it remains personal. My Gambian girlfriends describe the pain as a necessary part of the birth process. The fact that there are no painkillers available makes them afraid.

When I saw those posters on the hospital wall I laughed bitterly at the irony and at the huge gap that exists between the Western world and the shocking conditions in The Gambia. In the West, the chances of injury to mother or baby during a birth are almost non-existent, and usually very minor in comparison to what happens in developing nations. In The Gambia, for example, one of the more common damages can be injury to the vagina or pelvic floor. There is also a chance of a fistula, which is a tear between the birth canal and the ovaries. This occurs during the birth and can be the result of poor hygiene or nutritional deficit. A fistula will cause the woman to be unable to control her bodily functions, and urine or feces may drip continuously. This is a common occurrence in The Gambia and other developing nations, causing untold suffering both on a physical and emotional level. It often leads to a woman becoming a social outcast and then committing suicide.

Very young girls are subject to vaginal injury from forceful sexual entry, vaginal circumcision, unprofessional abortions, and from midwives, nurses and doctors who are not trained to deal with long or complicated births. Many defects are caused by poor nutrition, bad sanitary conditions, genetic mutations not tested for, or undetected problems during pregnancy. In the West, the rate of defects in newborns is much, much lower, but the fear of having a deformed baby is still largely present and is often expressed along with a feeling of helplessness during pregnancy and labor.

The feelings of helplessness feed the fear, and vice versa. Women whom I guide through pregnancy and delivery in Israel speak of their fear of loss of control during the birth. That the process will be taken over by the medical team. Often, I hear about an uncaring staff member who does not listen to the birthing mother's requests and treats her as unimportant to the whole procedure.

Sometimes I meet women before their delivery who are scared of their midwife. She has said unkind words to them, or insisted upon intrusive tests that the mother did not agree to or had downright refused.

Western women are often afraid of the effect of the birth on their mental health. I have never heard such a fear expressed in Gambia, or in any other tribal or traditional society that I have visited. It seems that if you have to struggle just to stay alive, encroachment on your personal freedom or mental stability is not a priority concern. This would seem to explain the fact that post-natal depression is almost unheard of in traditional societies.

In The Gambia, fear ignites women to act. To act without ceasing, and use every means at their disposal to try and lessen the threats and dangers to the fetus. They look for and develop techniques to cope with their fears. The techniques they have invented vary according to circumstances. Every human or animal who is threatened will fight back and attack, or run away. Sometimes they will become passive – ignoring the threat in the hope that the danger will pass them by.

The Gambian women I met seemed to deal with the dangers of the upcoming birth by clinging to the sisterhood. In The Gambia, a woman lives every minute of her life in the company of other women. They work together, raise the kids together, cook together, sleep together (sometimes in the same bed), and are almost never apart. A woman will not want to do anything that is not in accordance with the customs of her community.

Together they seek ways of earning money so that they will be able to afford to go to a private birth clinic run by Europeans. This would greatly improve the chances of survival for their baby. They work tirelessly to prepare and sell food in the market or even prostitute themselves to wealthy tourists. Once the child is born, they may in desperation give him up to someone else in the hope that he will now have a better chance of survival.

Community life and mutual aid are their main tools for dealing with hardship, giving them a sense of security and safety. Women live together, protecting one another. They also protected me. Anna Gaye, for example, accompanied me on my trip to learn the secrets of African baby massage, in order to keep me safe and to advise me. She agreed to return to Serrekunda only when she was certain that I was safe and protected.

The women have a shared economy, watch each other's children and share in each other's joys and misfortunes. Shared parenthood of all the children in the compound is part of the tapestry of life. The women know that if some tragedy should befall one of them, the other women will care for her children. This removes the fear that they will be orphaned and gives some comfort.

They cook together and gather water together from the well or nearest tap. This sharing of tasks eases the hardship of daily manual labor. Everyone also tries to earn money for the extended family to survive, and they are partners in the struggle for a decent life. If one woman in the compound decides to open a food concession, all will enlist to help her in the project.

This communal lifestyle is not merely a matter of choice. In order to make sure that everyone pulls his/her weight for the common good, there is a system of checks and balances. Input is constantly measured, and tabs kept on how much and in what way each has contributed to the welfare of the group. The deep-rooted belief in magic and the power of spells also helps to keep the society intact. It is the force that keeps everyone on the right track of helping others. For example: Today I will help you, so that you will not be angry and put a curse on me, and tomorrow you will help me for the same reason.

In this way cooperation is ensured, and in the long run it enables the community to function optimally under very harsh living conditions. The women obey the laws of community half-willingly and half-fearfully, but the chances of the group's survival are improved.

The option of being able to resort to magic that can change someone else's life dramatically gives a feeling of power and reduces fear,
even though their life has so few other choices. When something
bad happens and is understood to have been caused by magic, it is
not just a random event. It also gives people a sense of control over
what happens in life.

The French anthropologist Claud Levi-Strauss describes magic
as an instrument for coping with the dangers of childbirth. In his
essay "Uses of Symbols" he explains a song of magic that is sung in
the Kone tribe of South America. The song tells of a woman going
through a difficult and dangerous labor. A local shaman helps the
woman to overcome the complications, and explains that she suffers
because she has lost her *forba* (her spirit double who is in charge
of her life force.) The Kong believe that a difficult delivery occurs
because the '*moh-o* (spirit in charge of creating the fetus) oversteps
its role and traps the *forba*.

The shaman and the benevolent powers that surround him will
combat the *moh-o* until it releases the mother's *forba*. Then the birth
can take place. The shaman does this with song, healing plants, and
other means. He works to create a dialogue between the *moh-o* and
the physical and spiritual forces of the woman. The struggle will not
be to overcome the *moh-o*, because the *moh-o* is a necessary agent
for fertility. The battle is only against the unrestrained use of her
power and authority.

Once the battle is concluded and the mythical figures (the *moh*-o
and her helpers) understand that they have overstepped their boundaries, only then does the shaman give orders to the benevolent and
balancing forces to act. When the *forba* returns to her proper place
inside the woman, her vital energies will now return and she will be

able to overcome the enemies and the pain. The womb (home of the *moh-o*) can also return to its full strength.

According to Levi-Strauss's analysis, the shaman uses techniques similar to those of psychoanalysts. He listens to what the mother in labor is saying and echoes it back to her. In this way, he raises the subconscious problems of the mother to consciousness, and by using mythology explains to her clearly the conflict that is going on inside her. He tells her about the relationship between her *forba* and *moh-o*, and that her *moh-o* has overstepped the boundaries of her role. He enables her to understand what is happening and this in turn allows her to gather her strength and overcome the situation.

The modern delivery room uses many kinds of equipment and tests to enable us to gather information that would otherwise be unknowable – to see things that are not visible to the naked eye and to hear things that our ears cannot hear. For example, a monitor will allow us to hear the baby's heartbeat, ultrasound enables us to see him, and blood tests can expose what is happening inside the fetus. The use of medical equipment is also supposed to mitigate the woman's fears –– at least to some extent.

This 'magic' is a sort of technological equivalent of mystical experience. It is possible to equate it to a shaman who 'enters' the woman's body and sees, hears, and perceives her experience. He is able to connect with different forces that are influencing the birth process. The actions of the shaman instill a feeling of control into the birthing mother and dispel her fear.

A modern Western woman is able to choose the type of birthing situation that she feels is safest and best for her, and where it will take place. She can choose who will be with her and has the option to learn about the process in an assortment of prenatal classes. All this serves to diminish her fear about the upcoming delivery.

Her social support system is completely different from that of her sisters in The Gambia. A Western woman will usually have a 'nuclear' family arrangement which, on the one hand, insulates her from the community, but on the other hand allows her to make personal choices. The Western woman's level of interaction with the community is entirely a matter of choice. Every entry to her personal space is regulated and chosen entirely by her.

The privacy given to her in the delivery room allows her some choice of whom will accompany and support her, but the space as a whole is unfamiliar and alien. She is often alone, before, during, and after the birth, which leaves her to cope on her own with her fears and insecurities about her situation.

Social support is a fundamental need, and for this reason virtual and many other types of communities have been created for the pregnant woman outside the nuclear family. These social structures are based on shared ideas and beliefs. Many of the support groups will help the pregnant woman gain trust in herself and her body, which makes her feel safer. Just the fact of being together with other women in these groups helps her to find her individual path. With the assistance of those whom she has chosen to be around her, she is able to go within herself and understand what frightens her and find solutions that suit her.

Pregnant women who are not afraid at all – worry me. Fear is important because it drives us to act. Fear prompts us to prepare for the unexpected with all the means at our disposal. It drives us to take actions that lower the danger threshold and increase our confidence in a sometimes unpredictable situation.

The tools used in the traditional world and the Western world are different, but they serve the same purpose – to make the birth mother stronger and more confident by giving her physical and emotional support, and a sense of control over the birth process. .

In The Gambia, the cohesion created by conforming to social norms and a life shared closely with others improves the chances of survival. Magical forces are called upon to deepen the ties of individuals to the community and to combat the many dangers that lurk.

The fears of Westerners during pregnancy and birth are similar to those in traditional cultures, but the coping strategies are different. The individualistic lifestyle of Westerners looks to acquiring knowledge about the process, using technologically advanced tests, and relying on personal support groups.

The processing of emotional states during pregnancy is important for us. We must check where our fears come from within us and how they are expressed. We can build a personal strategy according to individual needs to regain confidence and feelings of control.

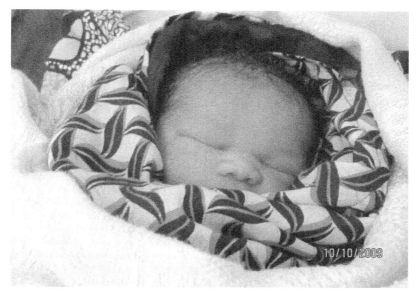

Albert

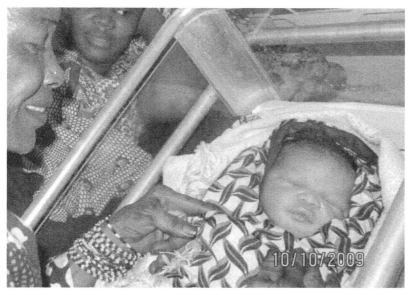

Anna-gei and new Albert

Anna-gei cooking in the yard

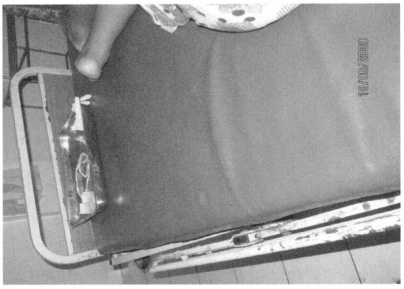

Birthing bed in the hospital in Banjul, the capital of Gambia

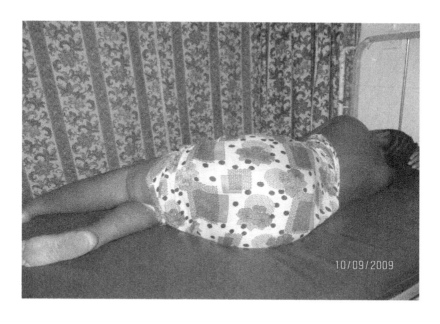

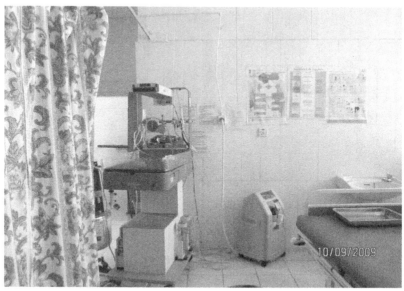

Hippo in the river Baboon Island

Massaging the baby

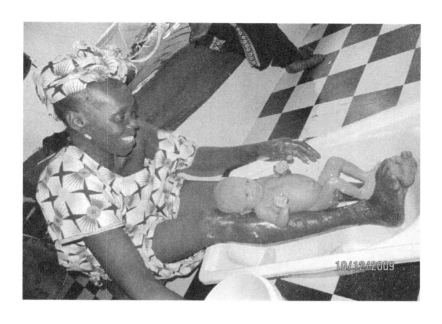

Baboon Island

Anna-gei and new Albert

To the market - Banjul

India - Hierarchy

The floor of Delhi airport is covered with brown carpet and the sound of vacuuming reverberates in the background. With a long steady hum, the dust of many roads is sucked into large round containers.

A sculpture stands at the entrance to the terminal. A gigantic spiral that touches the carpet and snakes up and up. On it are 12 figures in bronze representing the twelve *asanas* (positions) in the salutation to the Sun. The palms of Buddha gesture at me from the walls and two statues of elephants also welcome me. They are the symbol of Ganesha, the God of all beginnings. He is responsible for the formation and removal of obstacles and also for success and prosperity. Strands and engravings of silver bless my arrival.

"Namaste to you too," I say to the bronze characters, "thank you for the greeting."

India says to me, "You have landed in an ancient culture, even if things here seem new and modern."

Another two airports and a day later I sit in a small office in Bangalore, across from Dr. Sudarshan. He is 65 years old and is wearing a clean white button-down shirt.

"You cannot come here for such a short time, learn a bit about something and then practice it," he says after I explain to him that I wish to learn from traditional midwives. "For example, herbal remedies are a deep and serious subject. Do you promise you will not use what you learn in a slip-shod manner?"

"I promise."

In the middle of the jungles of Karnataka state, Dr. Sudarshan has set up a medical center which uses a combination of new medical methods and the wisdom of the nomadic tribes who have lived in the dense mountainous jungles of Dakkan for thousands of years as hunter gatherers. Their traditional midwives and other healers were entrusted with knowledge by their ancestors. Knowledge about the use of medicinal plants and leeches for healing that has been passed down for generations.

As someone who came from a traditional Indian family which respected and appreciated tribal wisdom, Dr. Sudarshan decided to dedicate his life's work to helping and learning from the tribal people. He first made contact with an elderly midwife named Sidama, who helped tribal mountain women at births. He would accompany her and her daughter, giving support and help when needed at the more complicated deliveries. He learned from Sidama the secrets of traditional healing, and after her death continued to work with her daughter Jara Maadama, who succeeded her.

In the 1970s Dr. Sudarshan founded the Vivekananda clinic in one of the British summer towns in the Biligiriranga Hills. It lies in the midst of cool jungle, many gruelling hours journey from Bangalore. Alongside his medical clinic he built a school and began teaching children to read and write. Until then, children were thought of only as a labor force. To encourage the parents to send their kids to school, every child who came received a bag of rice that day. Today Dr. Sudarshan lives in Bangalore and supervises from afar the project he began.

After the meeting with the Doctor I begin my journey to the clinic. I am squashed on a little bench on the rickety bus. I can barely breathe because of the people pressing against me and the heat. Every inch of the bus is packed with people, packages, chickens and a goat. People hang on outside with calloused hands. The driver sits in a large seat padded with rags. A long gearshift sticks out of the floor and twists under his expert hand. I yell my destination to him in English and over the mass of heads between us. I see him wobble his head from side to side and smile at me in the mirror. Yes, he will let me know.

The bus climbs up the mountains on a bad road through the jungle. Once in a while it stops and people get off and on, but the bus remains fully packed at all times. Only the faces change. Everyone smiles when they see me, their heads wag and their eyes stare. Six hours later, seemingly endless and filled with many jolts, curves, hooting horns, and sweat, the bus grinds to a halt. We are on an open clearing in the middle of the dense jungle and a few huts can be seen from the window. The driver turns to me and everyone looks. "B.R. Hills!" he announces.

I get down onto the dirt road and the bus departs, leaving a huge cloud of dust in its wake. I make my way towards the school, and Dr. Sudarshan's appointed deputy receives me there with a kind face and respectful manner. The school is out of session and many pupils have gone home, so I am appointed a room in the students' quarters. A small bungalow made from basalt (lava stone), with a cement floor and a little window with a screen. Deluxe conditions and I'm grateful they have thought in advance about mosquitos. The bed is rusty iron with a board on top, a very thin mattress and even thinner blanket. There is no bathroom, just a hole in the yard. In BR Hills there is no running water. The pail of water I received was special guest treatment.

It is already noon and the energetic deputy invites me to join him in the dining room. At the entrance children wait for lunch. Outside the door are narrow shelves and on them, in exceptional orderliness, are placed pairs of flip-flops, shoes and sandals. All are very well worn. The children stand barefoot, one after the other, in a tidy line. Each holds a tin plate as they silently file into the big room.

The walls painted a faded and peeling sky blue. On the cement floor long mats are placed along the walls, on which the children sit silently with their legs crossed. They steal curious glances at me and try to be polite and suppress their laughter.

A loud screeching is heard as giant steel pots are dragged across the floor. Deep grooves carved into the cement show that many have been dragged before. The people on work duty move from child to child serving rice with sauce spooned over it. I receive a plate and sit with the staff: Dr. Niha – the doctor who manages the center – and Angeli and Dipika, two student doctors who have come here to do their internship from the University of Bangalore.

The staff receives its food on banana leaves, as do most simple Indian people. This is a case of hierarchy in reverse, but there is no room for error, and the respect shown to the staff is obvious. A young boy blesses the food in Sanskrit and everyone repeats it after him.

We eat in silence. I try to eat with my hands like everyone else but it drips all over me. My nose is also dripping from the burning spicy hot food on my tongue and hands. My face is red and my lips are on fire, but I am hungry and it is very tasty. The kids try not to laugh at this foreign woman in strange clothes who is dripping and whining with eyes tearing and barely managing to get the food into her mouth. The laughter gets louder and I laugh along.

"When he first arrived here, the jungle inhabitants did not understand what he wanted," the doctor next to me says. "Dr. Sudarshan grew up in a high caste family and came here as part of his studies. He had a highly developed sense of justice and this was what motivated him to build his small clinic here. The tribal people would peek and run away. They wanted to continue their traditional ways. It took him a long time to convince them that he was on their side and his objective was to help. He wanted to give their children some education so that they could fit into modern life, and for everyone to be able to receive proper medical care.

After lunch she invites me to come with her to the clinic. It's a single-storey mud building with no door. About 10 people are already waiting for her by the doorway. They are dressed in tatters that once were pants and shirts. Their hair is wild and they don't seem to have bathed for some weeks. Their skin is very dark, sunburnt and creased. Inside the clinic, shelves along the walls hold some medical equipment. Everything is old but clean.

Dr. Niha welcomes the first patient with a smile. He is a man with some teeth missing, whose age I cannot even guess at. His hands are calloused and his eyes black and feverish. He is from the Soliga tribe. He is reluctant, but the doctor calms him and manages to take his blood pressure and listen to his heart and lungs with a stethoscope. She sends him to the next room to receive his medication.

"He should stay here," she says, "but he probably won't agree to that. Sometimes I think I have succeeded in convincing a patient by telling him that if he stays here he can get treatment that will save his life. But the next day I find out that he preferred to die in the forest rather than to spend a night here.

"You must understand that the culture of these people sanctifies nomadic life and they do not trust any permanent structure." She tells me that the Soliga tribe, like the other tribes around here, live as hunter gatherers. "They move from place to place according to the seasons and where they can find food. It is not possible for them to store food for any length of time, so when their food is finished, they move to another place. When they leave one area the ground has a chance to rest, the trees grow back, and the animals reproduce and replenish. If in another season the conditions are right, they might return to the same place again. The tribal groups are small and have no system of hierarchy."

When I hear this I am amazed. "What do you mean? There is no one in charge of the group? No leader?"

"No," she says. "There is only division of labor but it is not based on worth. No single job is considered more important than another. In the traditional hunter gatherer society the hunter who brings home the meat does not touch it himself. It is divided among the people of the tribe and the hunter waits for his share. Sometimes the tasks are shifted around. The few possessions that they own and the meat of the hunt belong equally to all."

The tribal people of this area did not have contact with the outside developed world until the people with money arrived (the British). They began to buy up sections of the jungle and to cut down the trees. The tribal people found themselves with less and less area to move around in. Today the government tries to resettle them in permanent villages, but even after years of living in these settlements the jungle people remain highly suspicious of modern innovations and especially of the medical system.

"The thing is," says Dr. Niha, "that jungle people were very rarely ill, and today they are more so, due to unhealthy foods and a way of life no longer in accord with the seasons as they were used to."

Towards evening the line of patients becomes shorter.

The doctor takes me to see the "birthing center." She pulls aside a curtain at the end of the room and Voila! Here is a small room, one bed, an old-fashioned baby scales and some bottles with medical equipment. In two corners of the room are niches. One contains a bucket for a shower and the other has a hole in the floor for a toilet. The walls are covered with blue ceramic tiles and in the middle of the room a thick rope is suspended from the ceiling. Dr. Niha explains that women who prefer to squat can hold on to the rope for support.

On the wall a big poster has writing on it in the local language. It says that whoever gives birth at the center will receive a very large amount of money from the government. The amount is almost an entire year's salary in this region. If you have twins, you receive double. If you have your baby at home you receive nothing. This system of reward and punishment is of course very successful in getting women in India to give birth in hospitals.

When I ask Dr. Niha about the practical methods she uses to reduce labor pains, she answers as I was answered in Alaska, Madagascar, and South Dakota: "What do you mean? Birth is painful." End of story.

"In addition to deliveries we are busy educating women about general health." The doctor tells me this as we walk on the path from the medical center to the classrooms. Young women from the surrounding villages are waiting for us. They come to learn about hygiene, such as brushing your teeth, birth control, and much more. This project is funded by the government. Today the class is about women's physiology – the structure of the uterus, conception and pregnancy. I also take part in the discussion and the women seem to be listening and paying attention.

Night is falling as I am accompanied by three of the young women who were instructed to take care of me. The noises and smells of the forest are all around us as we walk down the path to my room. As soon as we have said good-bye, I close my door I lie down on the bed. I fall asleep listening to the rustling of leaves and animals and the wings and cries of night birds in the living jungle.

The next day I join Dr. Niha and her mobile hospital on a trip into the jungle. It's a white jeep with a Red Cross sign painted on it. The medical staff travel in the jeep to give treatments to people of the Soliga tribe who are not used to leaving their jungle habitat. Today the staff are going to inoculate children against local diseases. Tourists are forbidden to enter here and the staff made great efforts to get me permission to come with them.

After about an hour's drive we stop. A dark woman with shining eyes, wearing a colorful sari, comes out to meet us from within the dense jungle. She has a smile from ear to ear on her face. This is Jerra Ma'adama. We do not share a common language but we both begin to laugh. Dr. Niha translates for me and says that Jerra will take me to meet a young woman about to give birth any day now. Before that we will go to the Sacred Tree. As we walk along the jungle paths, Jerra points out footprints of elephants and warns me that if we meet with elephants I must be completely still until they leave. If they feel at all threatened they may attack, especially if very young elephants are among them. They are very protective of their young.

But I hope that we meet some.

We arrive at the foothills of the mountain, take off our shoes and proceed barefoot to the Sacred Tree. The whole area is sacred, Jerra explains matter of factly. Her eyes constantly scan the jungle. She does not have to look at her feet, they know the way by themselves.

She bends down and picks a leaf, crushes it and gives it to me to smell. Dr. Nira tells me its name in English but I do not know it. Jerra explains that it is used as an antiseptic for wounds.

My feet hurt. Walking barefoot is difficult for me. The path winds around and leads us to a large clearing. In the center stands a huge tree. Around it are piles of stones painted in many colors, and what look like tridents are stuck into the ground and decorated with branches of lemons.

In India, trees have always been close to the hearts of the people, Jerra says. They were considered as members of the family. Trees are the children of the Gods, and the trees in turn comfort and protect humans. She stands under the tree and gives me a bunch of leaves to smell. "The trees give without expecting anything in return," she says. "That's how it should be in a family and so it was among us when we lived in the jungle. We knew that we would always have whatever we needed because it belonged to all of us." She strokes the tree as she speaks.

She draws a red dot between my eyes. She gathers leaves and stacks them at the foot of the tree. She arranges some stones into a pile. She dips her finger into the bag that contains the red dye and paints the stones with dots and lines. She sticks fresh lemons on the points of the tridents, pours water on my head and blesses me. We circle round the tree. She gives me a piece of colored cloth and signals with her head toward the tree, and I tie my piece of cloth among the many others that blow in the wind.

The trident is the symbol of Shiva. His function in the world is to destroy the threefold world of matter, tradition, and religions, all of which are based on actions and sensations, in order to make way for the creation of a unified blissful world.

We continue on our way – with shoes. Giant cicadas shriek around our ears and everything in the jungle is alive and moving. Enormous butterflies float around us, and once in a while Jerra points out a large termite nest hanging in a tree, or a lizard running on the trail. She knows every path and plant here and walks light-footedly and easily between the thorny brambles. All the while, she gathers seeds, flowers and plants along the way and puts them somewhere inside her sari. She mentions that there are many plants in India used to ward off evil or remove curses.

Later she will prepare medicine that she learned to make from her mother, who learned from her mother, who learned from her mother. Dr. Niha shows me the black cumin seeds (*sajeera*) and explains that she too uses the extract made from these seeds to stop bleeding during births at the clinic.

The woman who is due to deliver is waiting for us in her hut. She looks not more than 14, but it turns out that this is her third birth! The hut is made of mud, with an earthen floor. Between two of the walls a bamboo pole is stretched with a sari hanging on it and a rug on the floor below.

Jerra speaks to her in dialect and the woman says that she has been having contractions for some hours now. In my heart I thank my lucky stars for this opportunity to see Jerra in action. The young woman speaks with the midwife while arranging the pile of mattresses, pieces of cloth, and clothes for the newborn. Every once in a while she stops and after a minute continues with what she was doing. It's a little hard to see what is going on because the room is dark, with only a shaft of light coming through the cracks between the mud walls and the ceiling.

The mother-to-be sits on the floor and Jerra exposes her belly to palpate the uterus, verifying that the baby is on the way. In the yard a fire is lit and a pot of water put on to boil. Jerra takes a bottle of castor oil from the folds of her sari and pours some onto the girl's belly.

Dr. Niha explains to me that this tells Jerra how the birth will unfold. If the oil runs quickly in a straight line down from the navel, the birth will be quick and easy. If it runs slowly down the sides of the belly, the birth is expected to be long. From this diagnosis she will know what plants she needs, if any, and which prayers to recite. I try to find out how the direction of the oil tells how the birth will proceed, but Dr. Niha doesn't know and doesn't ask the midwife. It could be that the oil indicates how the baby is positioned in the pelvis, and runs straight down the belly if it is in the correct position.

Jerra makes tea from the cumin seeds, and the excited young intern who is with us listens with a stethoscope to the birthing mother's heartbeat and to the baby's heartbeats as well. The midwife massages the mother's back and speaks soft words of encouragement to her. When the pains become stronger and the good and strong contractions begin, Jerra guides the woman over to the hanging sari. She almost doesn't have to tell her what to do, as she already knows. She holds on to the sari and begins to squat. With every contraction she squats a bit lower until she arrives at a sitting position on the rug. I can scarcely breathe with anticipation.

The woman moans from deep in her throat and strains, making a great effort. Jerra rolls up her sari sleeves and the baby's head appears at the opening. Another few minutes and the baby is in her hands. She places the baby on the mother's stomach. The mother is now leaning against the wall of the hut. She wipes him and announces that it's a boy. We all giggle with happiness. In India a boy baby is preferable and the Mom is happy too.

Two minutes later Jerra ties off the umbilical cord with two strings, cuts between the two strings with a sharp knife and burns the end with a candle flame. The placenta comes out after a few minutes and (as in Madagascar and Alaska) the afterbirth will be buried deep in the ground. According to their beliefs, if a dog or other animal finds and eats the placenta, the baby will come to harm.

Jerra is concerned that the bleeding is too heavy and Dr. Niha steps into the picture. She presses on the belly to check if the uterus has shrunk properly. She takes a vial of Pitocin out of her bag and gives it to the intern to inject. Meanwhile, Jerra prepares tea from the black seeds and roots of *khikaki*, a species of acacia. This tea is good for stopping the bleeding and also for helping the mother's milk, the intern explains. The new mother lies down on the mattress with the baby next to her. Her other children come in to visit and neighbors join us, bringing tasty and spicy food.

Jerra does not accept any money, the doctor tells me. The people pay her in food, just as in the ancient Vedic tradition. According to The Vedas, the wise teachers are representatives of God on earth and their wisdom belongs to everyone. Jerra is only a channel through which the knowledge comes down. It is not her property and she cannot ask for payment for it.

In the evening I take leave of the very special women I have come to know, and await the bus that will take me back to Bangalore. The bus comes into view around the bends in the road. It is full of people and to my great surprise Jerra is sitting in it! She clears a way for me through the passengers. Everyone knows and respects her. She gives me her huge smile, touches my face, and blesses me with her eyes. After a few kilometers the bus stops and Jerra signals me to get off with her. Everyone looks at us and waits. She hugs me, touches my face again, and blesses me. I hug her in return and get back onto the bus with tears in my eyes.

I am now going to Cochin, which is on the west coast. The day passes in traveling and I find myself on the night train, swaying to the rhythm and noise of the wheels, the blasts from the engine, and the cries of the vendors who move from car to car offering snacks. Eyes stare at my face without a shred of inhibition or embarrassment. The smiles are hesitant at first, and get wider when I smile back. The compartment is full of passengers sitting close together. Some climb up and sit on the high shelves used for luggage. Thankfully, a few people make room for me on a bench. Many people are standing in the aisles. It is very crowded and everything seems to be in motion.

Hours go by with scenes passing before my eyes. Around me is constant chatter, and little by little I get to know who is who and the relationships between them. A couple with a young child and the man's mother. A father and son on a work trip. A grandmother and grandfather with round faces. Long black, gray braids are wrapped around some heads and hanging loose on others. Men dress in traditional clothes or Western attire. Sadhus (religious ascetics) dress in orange robes and Sikhs have turbans. There are shaven heads and people wearing hats.

A student with her family on the way to a wedding is happy to practice her English with me. Conversations are happening all around us. The children take up most of the attention. Everyone takes part in caring for them and keeping them occupied. A young mother unwraps and offers her one-year-old baby some food from her bundle. He opens his little mouth and takes the food that she has pre-chewed for him. When he pees in his pants, the mother undresses him, washes the pants out the window and hangs them to dry in the wind.

After feeding the baby she feeds her husband. He sits there using his phone and she puts food piece by piece into his mouth with her fingers. The baby passes from hand to hand between the passengers. Everyone is busy eating and talking. The baby becomes tired, so a man sitting on the top shelves ties a sari from shelf to shelf, tests its strength, and thus creates a hammock for the baby to be rocked in, swaying to the rhythm of the train and the noise of the passengers.

The hefty grandmother who is certainly the boss of one family, gives orders to her granddaughter and eats the entire time. She tells me that she and her large brood are en route to a sacred ceremony in a village near the next train stop. The ceremony is held for people who wish for a baby and those who want to thank the goddess Durga for the baby they have received. They will stay around the Temple of the goddess Durga and bring her offerings of thanks and/or prayers for fertility.

I decide to change my plans and join them. I get off the train surrounded by families and their belongings. In the distance I can see bright flags waving in the breeze and tents made from colored cloths spread out around the man-made lake full of murky water and lotus leaves. Upon arriving, I see that between the tents are huts containing cooking gear, crates of cloth, mattresses and blankets. Enough equipment for a month. The cloths are embroidered with elephants of crimson and gold, and it seems to me that this entire temporary camp has been organized solely for my benefit.

People have come from all over the country to sleep under the stars for an entire month of festivities. They will rise everyday with the sun, and two members of each family will place long poles of sugarcane on their shoulders with a sari tied between them in a makeshift litter, to transport their newborn son or daughter. The whole family marches along to the temple, which is covered with glittering lights. Everyone sings and dances and makes a lot of noise.

Outside the camp, bearers carry palanquins (litters) engraved with geometric designs and embroidered with beads. Elephants trumpet sounds far and wide when they pass by with their drivers, while young boys run swiftly up and down their tusks.

The alleyways around the temple are full of people and vendors who shout their wares. There are balloon stands, and toys and noisemakers are on sale too and of course all kinds and colors of foodstuffs. In the center of the main street is a shelter for the VIPs, before whom passes an endless parade of entertainers. There are musicians with drums and trumpets and a great number of people. Some hold round clay vessels containing fire. Some hold offerings to the goddess, which can be rice, bananas, incense sticks, fruits, orange and white flowers and paper notes. Some carry small statues of gods on their heads or in their arms. There is a cacophony of noise and commotion from tambourines and trumpets, horns beeping, drums and voices singing. Crazy music blasts from huge loudspeakers as well, and the whole procession sways and dances.

I join the parade.

In their saris, women do cartwheels and somersaults in the air, landing back into the mud and slime. They do this for hours and are covered in mud. They give themselves up to Mother Earth and to the grace of the dance. They come to ask and pray for fruit in their wombs. Perhaps their prayers will be answered and next year they will arrive to show their baby to the goddess, to give thanks and to bless others who need her help.

Immediately after the women come the fire dancers. Some hold round rings of iron containing bowls of fire. People shower them with holy water. Others have long spears stuck into the flesh around their waists. They impale themselves over and over in the blazing heat, but no blood flows.

The euphoria grows and grows and everyone now joins the

parade, dancing and singing, all flowing towards the glowing coals that are spread out at the entrance to the Temple. The praying masses will walk across more than four yards of sizzling embers in their bare feet. They are in an altered state of consciousness and without any hesitation tread on the burning ground, suffering no burns or wounds.

I am filled with emotion and covered in sweat when I finally step out of the thundering crowd and return to the campsite.

Lengths of cloth separate each family's territory, and every family has a small fire burning with pots of food bubbling away on it. There are children everywhere and in the corners are piles of papers, feces, feathers, bags, bones, and peels of all sorts. Women are busy cooking, washing clothes, nursing babies, and shooing away dogs, cats and flies. There is a lot of noise and bustling about, but everything runs smoothly and peacefully, no one yells and there is no arguing.

The family I came off the train with invites me to sleep with them. From the cooking fires, smells of food and smoke waft through the air. Music can still be heard from the distant parade ground and in addition every family tent has its own music. Along with the lights from the fires, little lamps hung on poles give out a pale light in the darkness.

In a melodic mix of Hindi and English, one of the family members explains to me that they tried for years to have a baby without success. A year ago they decided to come on this pilgrimage and pray to the Holy Goddess and look! The miracle occurred – he points to his nursing baby – here he is! We saved up money to come again this year to thank the goddess and to give her offerings.

The next day I change my plans once again. I decide to forget about Cochin and fly instead to the northeast of India to the Kullu Valley, in the middle of Himachal Pradesh in the western Himalayas.

Out is the name of a small village in the Valley of Banjar, which branches out from the Kullu Valley. My guide here is named Farakash. He's a tall, thin man who greets me with a happy face at the hut where I will sleep for the next few days. The houses here are built from black slate supported by wooden beams. This style of building is very old and effective, and the houses stand for many, many years.

Farakash guides me on the paths through the forest to meet Remi, the midwife who was present at his own birth. I am wearing high shoes and using walking sticks. The ground smells of dampness and the earth is muddy and dark. The smells of the forest seem to contain the odor of clothes hung to dry in the wind and the scent of flowering apple trees, along with the dark earthen smell.

I move within the silence of the great green mountains. "Go slowly, Madam," says Farakash. He treats me with great respect and worries that I will over-exert myself. We arrive at a pool of water surrounded by slate. A man in traditional clothing – wide pants, a button-down shirt with a vest over it – takes off his sandals and goes down the steps to the muddy water. He cups his hands and takes a drink. Farakash tells me these are holy waters, healing waters. The water comes from the monsoon and passes deep through the belly of the earth gathering minerals on its way here.

The man leaves us. His hat is shaped like a straight-sided pot and Farakash explains that it shows that he comes from the Valley of Kinnaur, to the northeast. The hat's green trim is the emblem of our valley, he explains with pride.

At the side of the road is a small building with a niche in its wall. In the niche stands a statue made of slate. At the feet of the statue are withered flowers, a dish of rice, some black bananas, incense sticks, red powder, pieces of gold and red cloth. These have been placed there by people who pass by. Farakash hands me a small piece of slate from the path and tells me to throw it on the pile of rocks next to the small temple. "It will bring you luck," he says. "It informs the gods that you have been here and you may make a wish."

I kneel down and throw the rock. I wish for health and happiness for all the people I love, and that this journey will deepen my knowledge about birthing.

We continue to walk down along the path until a village comes into view beyond the forest. Across from us, at the top of the path, some young women are going up. They are wearing colorful decorated hats and trousers with typical Indian tunics and vests knitted from light brown local wool. One of the women bends before Farakash and kisses the tip of his shoe. He touches her left shoulder with his right hand, and explains that this is the local custom upon meeting someone from your own extended family – the younger will kiss the shoe of the elder. All the other women greet only with eye contact. Using this small ritual makes it clear to everyone who is in the family, and who is older and deserving of respect. These clear distinctions safeguard the family structure.

The village where Dai ('midwife' in Hindi) Remi lives consists of a group of houses on a steep hill. They are piled one on top of another like layers of a cake, and each is surrounded by a veranda of carved wood. A flight of stairs leads to the entrances. Farakash says that I will not be able to enter the house because I am not of the same caste as the tenants.

"But I am not from here!" I protest, "I do not belong to any caste."

"That is the way here," he answers.

"So how come I am allowed in your house?" I persist.

"That is how I earn my living. I house people and am their guide, so it is permitted."

This incident helps me to clarify our relationship and to bring home the fact that I am a stranger and boundaries must be kept.

The midwife looks at us from her porch and then comes down to meet us. We all sit outside on the damp earth, surrounded by a multitude of flowers and wild canna bushes. Her eyes are very large and brown and she has no teeth. Each nostril bears a jewel in gold and she has earrings and a colorful head scarf. Our eyes meet in curiosity and we smile. Farakash introduces me and tells her that I work with pregnant women, and have come to learn about ways of birthing that were used in the past and perhaps are still used in certain places.

Dai Remi explains that a midwife here called *yorgen*, which means 'a woman with power from the goddesses' and my heart skips a beat. Here, as in other parts of the world, the word midwife relates to profound feminine power and has deep implications in different cultures. Her task includes that of supporting and mothering the woman in labor.

In Judaism the word for midwife is *chaya*. It means life (*chayim*), but also relates to the word for animals (*chayot*) and to the life force (*koach hahayim*). A midwife is considered to be someone who can see the newborn both as a physical and a spiritual being. She is responsible for calming the mother, as can be seen in the Bible, when. the midwife calms Rachel during the birth of Benjamin by telling her that she is having a son.

In French, a midwife is 'sage-femme' or wise woman, and 'the one who hears on the other side of the door.' In Germany she is also called Weise Frau. In English the word is derived from the Anglo-Saxon 'mid' meaning 'with' and 'wyf' meaning 'woman,' indicating that she is the one who is *with* the woman in labor. In Malagasy, *rinanzaza* means 'mother of the baby' and refers to the

Big Mother – the Mother of All.

The rumor has got around that a strange woman has arrived in the community, and women and girls start appearing from all over the village. They look at me laughingly with their large eyes. Some reach out a hand to touch me. The *yorgen* also touches my head and asks me why my hair is short. She touches my arms and feels my hands. She asks why I have spots on the backs of my hands.

She became a midwife relatively late in life, at the age of 40. She says there were many birthing guides in the region and only when she was 40 did the need arise for more. Her mother taught her the work.

In a relaxed manner, Remi begins to tell me some things that her mother taught her. It is important for a pregnant woman to eat a lot, but not heavy foods. After the birth she should eat meat and a lot of ghee (clarified butter, which is considered to be a food with many healing properties). If the birth is taking a long time, the woman in labor should be given hot water with *segira*. She shows me the black cumin seeds. Remi asks one of the women something and she hurries off, returning with a jar of oil. I smell the oil and guess "Almond?"

"No, it is the oil of apricot kernels (seeds). I massage her with this and it helps with the pain."

I have come to understand that in every area local products are used to make the necessary potions and remedies. The purpose of those used specifically for birthing women, provide easily available energy and warm her body with what is known in Sanskrit as *agni* – internal fire.

Remi explains that when delivery is close she checks the baby's position in the uterus. "If it is breech or transverse. I massage the belly very gently and ask the baby to turn around."

I ask her to demonstrate on me how she does this. She places her hand on my belly and strokes it lightly.

"That's it?" I ask in wonderment. That's the pressure you use for this action?"

She nods. "That is enough."

I am reminded of the custom of drawing on pregnant stomachs. Women draw drawings that describe the hidden baby or other drawings, and report that the baby feels the process and responds, but never that he turns his head down into the birth position. Perhaps here it is enough to give the baby a hint about which way to turn and he responds.

"Do you know the sex of the baby beforehand?" I ask.

"If he lies more on the left side of the uterus it's a boy and if on the right it's a girl. But it is forbidden to tell the mother-to-be," Remi answers.

In India it is preferable to give birth to boys. Girls create a financial burden on the family and are not wanted. The amount of women relative to men in India stands today at 600 women to 1000 men. In order to prevent proactive abortions of girls, strict laws were passed that impose heavy fines on whoever performs an abortion. This is why it is forbidden to disclose the sex of the fetus.

I ask Remi when she stopped assisting at births in the village and she flares with anger.

"I have not worked for many years already. I am not allowed. The government wants them to give birth in hospitals and the young women are confused and frightened. They have only one or maybe two children. In the hospital it is not good and they cut them." She performs the act of cutting in the air. "Many births end with an operation," she adds angrily. "In the hospital it hurts!"

"In hospital it hurts more?" I ask

"No," she states, and the women around us nod their heads. "It doesn't hurt at home because everything depends on the state of mind. In village births all the women will come and give their encouragement to the woman in labor. They will tell her that everyone does it, and she will not want to be embarrassed so she overcomes her pain."

"And if something happens?" I ask.

"It is karma," she answers.

"Sometimes a baby or a mother dies, sometimes there are problems that are beyond our strength. The gods decide."

In the same spirit, Remi says that she does not intervene in fertility problems. "If children do not come it is karma, it is from the gods. It is like rice. Rice always exists, but if there is a year with a bad harvest, that is karma, that's from the gods. The same with children."

I continue on my journey, heading north to the Valley of Kinnaur in Himachal Pradesh, to the village of Kalpa where most of the inhabitants are Buddhist. From afar I can see the snow-covered peaks of the Kinnaur Kailash mountain range. There are huge cedar trees and many apple orchards and other deciduous trees. Everyone's hat has green borders.

On the way we come across a group of women sitting together, crushing stones into gravel. I join them to learn how to hold the hammer and how much force to use, and how to be careful of the sharp bits of stone. A not-so-small crowd gathers around and everyone gives me advice. The talk turns to daily life, making a living, children, and of course, birthing. They ask me how many children I have and cluster to see the photos on my phone. I ask how many children they have and what their deliveries were like. The older ones say they gave birth in the village with the *dai,* the local midwife, the younger ones are silent.

I turn to one of the young women and ask her if she has children. Yes, she has two. She gave birth by Caesarean section each time. The other young women begin to open up and say they also gave birth this way. One by one they tell me. One had three operations, one had two. Only one of them gave birth twice, with no operation.

I continue to break stones and bang my fingers. I bite my lips, not to cry out.

"Why by operation?" I ask, and they look up at the sky, smile shyly, look at each other and say – that's what the doctor said.

I try to understand why there is such a high percentage of Cesarean sections. Different hospitals give different numbers, but it can be as high as 60%. The women say they agree to it because the doctor tells them to do it. I think that in the hospitals the women have no confidence in themselves nor anyone to protect them. They are isolated from the support of their families and friends, and their fear of the whole ordeal makes the pain worse. No one is there to massage their back and to give encouragement and tea. Anesthesia will be provided only if they agree to the operation, and because all other options of help are non-existent, they are left with no recourse, helpless and weak.

"Are you afraid?" I ask one of the young women who has not yet given birth. "Yes," she answers. "Very afraid."

"Why?"

She blushes and everyone looks at her.

"I am afraid that it will hurt and I am afraid of the operation. I know it hurts a lot."

These women work together, sharing the hardships of daily life. They help each other, gossip together, argue and laugh together. In the past, when one of them was about to give birth, she would know for certain that all of the other women would be there with her to encourage her to overcome the pains, and she would. That strong sisterhood has been torn apart since the births were forced out of the villages and into the hospitals.

In order to give birth in the hospital, the mother-to-be must travel a month in advance to the big city, either alone or with a female relative. The birth takes place in unfamiliar surroundings with strangers presiding, and without support from her closest friends and family.

I take my leave from these dear women and begin to make my way out of the village. In the middle of the path lies a hammer and I try to circle around it, but the women all cry out in alarm. I stop and look at them questioningly and they all laugh and tell my guide to explain it to me. It turns out that the hammer on the path is to remind passers-by to leave a tip for the workers, and I gladly pay my toll of passage.

I give them long hugs and continue my journey.

The road to Kalpa passes through Bhuntar, the big city of this region, and at one end of the city stands a hospital. A broken sign on its roof states its name and a few ambulances stand around. I tell the driver to stop and ask if I can visit the delivery room. He pulls up next to a woman in a nurse's uniform and they speak rapidly. After a few minutes I am putting on rubber gloves and following the nurse into the delivery room

In the room there are two beds, a very young midwife, a doctor and six young women in various stages of labor. There is not a word spoken or a sigh heard. The women sit on a bench along the wall, wearing their own traditional tunics and flip-flops. On the wall looms an eye-catching poster announcing that the government payments are only for those who give birth in the hospital, and not in the village.

A plump doctor wearing jeans and a white shirt signals to the women with movements of his head to get on the bed one by one so that he can check their progress. He wears a glove and a very serious expression as he performs the internal exams. One of the women groans during the exam and he places a comforting hand on her shoulder and smiles gently. She tries to smile back. When he finishes each exam, he explains to the midwife what stage of labor the woman is in.

Clearly it is the doctor who is king in the delivery room and everyone treats him with great respect. The mothers-to-be don't dare to address him and wait until he speaks to them. The midwives quickly obey any order he gives and lower their eyes when he speaks to them. Every word of his is esteemed as if out of the mouth of a god. His status as a doctor in India is very high, and he is regarded with unshakable respect because of his profession even if he was not born into a high caste.

For generations, India's social structure has divided people into clearly ranked categories that define how they earn a living and who they marry. The four main status groups are called Varnas in Sanskrit. The highest caste are the Brahmins, made up of priests and teachers. Next come the Kshatriyas, who are the rulers and warriors. Under them are the Vaishyas, who are farmers, tradesmen and craftspeople. The lowest caste are the Shudras, who are laborers and servants. One is born into a caste, and despite efforts to change the system over the past few centuries, there is minimal movement between castes.

A doctor's status is based on his profession and is not connected to the caste he was born into. He can be from different castes – except Shudras. When he takes care of a patient from a higher caste than his own, his standing as a doctor overrules the normal caste relations. No one here will ever question why the doctor decides what he does, and everyone treats him with great respect.

This attitude toward the medical system and doctors is not confined to India. Within the doctor–patient relationship the doctor always takes precedence. He is the one who knows, and he proposes the solution that will cure the disease. The status of a doctor as a 'possessor of knowledge' rises even higher as the knowledge about the human body develops. The "guild" opens to admit those who have the proper education. Those who have at their fingertips knowledge that is unseen to the naked eye – about germs, about the functioning of internal organs and systems and the chemical connections between medicine and disease.

This Western way of looking at disease stems from the underlying idea accepted today almost everywhere – that a disease is a problem that must be fixed. Since births are now performed in hospitals, they also are looked upon in this way: a problem in need of fixing. In order to 'fix' it the natural birth process is tampered with and the birthing woman is turned into a sick patient. Compared to the doctor she has no knowledge, and is placed in an isolated environment where she is looked upon as weak and suffering because of her 'illness.' The woman in labor expects Salvation from her caretakers and becomes passive. She is considered 'emotional' and her words and actions are not taken seriously. The birth and the woman become a matter of numbers and measurements.

In India, where a system of social hierarchy has long existed and is deeply rooted, this attitude toward birth is easily entrenched into the birthing mother. She is already an inferior being as a woman, and because of her lower caste, and this is now multiplied by her weakened state as a 'patient' before the all-knowing doctor. Women whom I met in India spoke with admiration and fear about doctors. "That's what the doctor said," was repeated every time the subject came up of how a birth took place..

The already weakened status of women is intensified when they must leave the safe and familiar space of the village and move near to the hospital, far from home, families and their usual social support system. In the hospital, the birthing women have no power whatsoever to contradict a doctor, because they do not understand the medical language. They do not even understand that they have the right to govern their own bodies. Their sense of powerlessness makes the fear of birth stronger. They have no choice but to give themselves over into the hands of the Great Deliverer.

In the Western world, this same hierarchy exists in hospitals. The doctor is in a superior position to the nurse or midwife, and has the final word about the correct treatment even if the midwife disagrees. Many times I have heard the woman or her husband declare that the doctor studied for so many years – "who am I to tell him what to do?"

When a woman arrives in the delivery room she understands its hierarchy perfectly well. She is the one in pain and in need of help and the medical staff are the ones in charge. This can also be seen in the hospital gown given to the patient, which is neither modest nor comfortable for giving birth, and by her physical position lying on the bed with the staff standing around and 'above' her, instead of sitting together with them in a discussion.

The woman in labor is 'forbidden' to detach herself from the machines and only the staff can regulate her through this specialized equipment and inform her what is going on inside her. The monitor records her contractions as if she does not know how and when they occur and at what strength.

The bed and the machines dictate how the birth will occur. For example, births can go very well if the woman is on all fours, on her hands and knees. In order for this to happen, the face of the midwife or doctor would be on the same level or lower than the woman's exposed rear end. In the Western world this will not happen, even though it might be the best position for the birth, because it would overturn the medical staff's dominant position over the woman, and threaten Western status norms.

I have heard over and over again of instances where the woman felt that the staff forced her to do some things she did not want to do. When women share their experiences of delivery rooms, their speech is punctuated with expressions such as "they told me to;" "the doctor decided for me, even though I wanted...;" "I was forced to...."

From their point of view, the medical staff want to help the woman. For example, they will offer to speed up a birth if it is not starting 'on time' or going according to schedule. In many hospitals women are advised to catalyze the birth after 41 weeks of pregnancy and at other hospitals they allow the woman to wait for a spontaneous opening until week 42. They will offer to break her waters if the contractions don't seem strong enough. If one of their measurements is not in line with another statistically, the staff will work to return the numbers to match the hospital's protocol.

The staff have one goal – to help the woman in labor. Within their belief system, the purpose of the medical staff and of the technology is to take active charge of the birth and push it forward, to help it to take place. Expressions such as "We want to help you," are very commonly heard in the delivery room and the meaning is clear: We do not trust that your body knows how to do this on its own, let us help you.

This attitude is prevalent in Israel and in the United States. But it is different in Holland, where the guiding principle is that the birth should be left to take place on its own unless there is an urgent need for intervention. The birth occurs in its own time and its own way, which suits both the mother and baby. No need to 'fix' anything that isn't broken.

Women behave in different ways upon entering the hierarchical medical sphere of the delivery room. Some accept the rules of the hierarchy and adopt those standards, believing that birth is a dangerous situation where medical intervention is necessary in order to overcome this. They see the doctors as persons of knowledge and authority and hand over responsibility for the birth to the medical team. Sometimes, however, this attitude is correct for the woman in labor. She yields to the system with confidence and peace, and this allows her to have a positive birth experience.

But in many cases the woman in childbirth does not know that there are alternative scenarios. Reality shows point the population in a certain direction – the one in which the medical team are the leaders, the decision makers, and the woman in labor is passive, allowing technology to save her and her baby.

There are also women who are proactive during their deliveries. They learn about the birth process and prepare themselves physically and emotionally, so that they can take responsibility for the birth of their own babies. During their pregnancy they learn about delivery room protocol and check out the different approaches of the doctors. They then choose the doctor and team that most suits their own approach. These women express their wants and needs, prepare a plan for the delivery to be the way they want it, and ask plenty of questions. They understand that by entering the medical system they are agreeing to some basic game rules, but at the same time they come equipped with basic tools and good communication skills to find a way of give and take, and will have a practical and meaningful dialogue within the system.

Then there are a growing number of Western women who are backing away from the hierarchical system and deciding to give birth at home. They prefer to give birth in familiar surroundings and choose professional women with experience who fulfill the criteria required by the Health Authority. These women trust in their own bodies, they are prepared, they are joyful and eager to experience the pains and effort of birthing. They learn different methods and gather tools to help them along the way.

The walls of the delivery room here in the north of India, that I enter quite by chance, are painted white, but have many stains from amniotic fluid, blood, and secretions from births that have taken place here before. On the wall, between the dirty stains, hangs a very clean and shiny picture of Krishna as a baby. He has round cheeks, light skin, and is colorfully decorated. The belief here is that if the woman looks at holy things during her labor, she will have an easy labor and the baby will be blessed.

Sweet Krishna with his kind eyes fills the room with his energy. He holds a flute – "chases after women," the midwife explains to me. He is leaning on a white cow, the Indian symbol for motherhood. Peacock feathers adorn both Krishna's head and the cow's head. Under the cow is another small figure of Krishna nursing from the cow's udder. The peacock symbolizes purity and the holy cow will influence the life of the newborn to always have plenty.

Under the picture, next to the check-up bed, stands a large garbage pail full of used gloves. The bed is covered with a red, fake leather sheet which is wet with fluid from one of the women whose water broke there. The midwife sneaks a glance at me and with an apologetic smile folds the dirty sheet in half. Here. She points to the bed, inviting the next mother-to-be to get up.

On the second bed a woman in childbirth holds the handles, purses her lips, arches her back. With her chest a little raised from the bed, she tilts her head backwards and pushes. The midwife performs a cut to her perineum and the woman lets out a low moan. When the baby's head appears the midwife helps her to come out. She pulls and swings her till the tiny girl is out, her new breasts pointing to the sky. The midwife quickly cuts the cord and wraps the baby in a colored cloth, and I am invited into the next room, where there is a bed for the newborn. The woman is left lying bleeding with her legs open in front of the other women.

In the next room they wipe the tiny baby and place her on a clean surface wrapped in a new blanket that the mother brought. She is weighed and placed under a warming machine. I stand next to the new baby. The sister-in-law and mother–in-law live near the hospital and have come to be with the baby. I wish her well, but my heart is bursting with emotion.

With a serious face, the doctor explains to me that he is very busy but will be happy to answer my questions.

"In one month 250 babies are born here. I have a staff of six midwives and I am the only doctor." He sighs. "The other doctor retired. Prenatal care includes blood tests and ultrasound once or twice during the pregnancy. If we find something is not right with the fetus we suggest to the parents to discontinue the pregnancy."

The women usually arrive here in active labor, so that the birth does not take long. They go through the long stages of contractions wherever they are staying, until they are ready to give birth. Usually I give them Pitocin to help, even if the labor is short. The midwives receive the babies. The cut is done at all first births. After the birth I listen to the baby's heartbeat to determine if he is all right.

I ask about the operations.

"If there is a long labor or if I suspect that something will go wrong, I perform an operation. Today, for example, I already performed four operations," he says.

After a normal birth the women stay in hospital for a few hours, or for one or two days after an operation. Immediately after a surgery an IUD is inserted into the uterus. These are government orders. I thank the doctor and go again to see the new baby girl. I am photographed with the family, take off my hospital slippers, put on my travelling shoes and leave the hospital.

Outside the hospital the usual commotion of the city is going on. Horns blast, trucks covered with brightly colored pictures and flashing lights snake through the traffic of innumerable bicycles, smoking motor bikes, and cars seemingly without brakes. We leave the city and return to the road that winds its way along the edges of the cliffs. I am now in the upper regions of the Himalayas in a village called Tabo, 4000 meters above sea level. We arrived after hours of travel on roads that circle ever upwards. The Himalayan peaks are immense and covered in snow. They look down on us on our winding roads amid the soaring cliffs.

It is hard to breathe because of the altitude, but also the difficulty of the road. It is very narrow, hammered out of the steep rock face. The curves are extremely sharp and buses, trucks and cars come face to face with us suddenly at high speeds. Deep down, far below us, I see icy rivers rushing through canyons.

Nab, the Buddhist guide who is accompanying me to Tabo, takes off his shoes at the entrance to the temple and raises his hands to his forehead. His eyes are closed. He mumbles prayers, bends his knee and lowers himself to the floor. He then stands up, and does this over and over again.

The young monks sit around wrapped in orange robes. One with a shaved head tells me about the various Buddhas and what can be asked of each one. The monks chant mantras in monotonous rhythm. The music enters into me, surrounds me, and little by little invades all the cells of my body. The smell of incense fills the space, which is decorated with figures of Buddha and depictions of his life. Outside the temple a huge golden statue of the Buddha sits gazing out across the plain in front of him, as he has done for hundreds of years. After a shared meal of warm, scented porridge with the monks, we leave the monastery.

The houses of the village are made of mud. The roofs are flat and covered with straw. The doors have white signs stuck on them with Hindi calligraphy and a drawing. "This protects the house," says Nab. "It explains to the devils and ghosts that they have come to the wrong place."

I meet with Rimpal the local Dai, a Buddhist midwife.

"Today is better," Rimpal says. "We used to work very hard and in the winter could not go anywhere, because the snow would cover up all the roads. We would sit all winter in the houses and weave." She points to the telephone in her house and says, "Once we all knew each other, but today we have distanced ourselves from one another and it is easier to keep in touch if there is a telephone."

I feel the woven materials she shows me. The wool is a light color with geometric designs and a border of red, blue and brown. Row upon row of interwoven threads tell of long cold days spent indoors weaving by candlelight.

"These are the wedding clothes of me and my husband," she says, draping the woven material against my neck and shoulders. "Here, you see, it looks good on you. Now you can marry again," she laughs. Even today, during the cold winter months, they weave. Even though there is electricity and water and telephones and it is possible to travel to nearby villages and also to the big city. "That makes us happy," she says and her eyes shine.

Rimpal is a small woman. Her face is criss-crossed with wrinkles. Her eyes are small and her nose points up. She seems full of the wind and the sun.

On the carved wooden shelves in her room are piles of books, covered with colored cloth dyed with saffron. The strong oranges and reds symbolize the search for truth. Small icons of Buddha, candles in copper candlestick holders, bowls of rice, flowers, peacock feathers and many other small ritualistic items are spread out on the table. Hanging above all this is the smiling Dalai Lama.

Rimpal was the village midwife for 15 years. Today the village women give birth at the medical center in the next town, about two days journey away. But in deep winter, when the roads are blocked with snow, the women will call Rimpal to help at the births. She explains to me and demonstrates on my back how she massages the sacrum of the woman in labor. Although she speaks in her language, I understand through my body how she lessens the pain. She very accurately touches exactly where the joints join together in the lower back.

She opens a Holy Book, smiles with her eyes full of warmth and light, and begins to hum and sing the Buddha's wisdom to me. I don't understand the words, but I hear the melody and by listening with my whole heart I feel the intention. When Rimpal finishes the songs by which she gives thanks to the Buddha for what there is and for whatever will be, she looks into my eyes and smiles.

"Yesterday was good," she says. "Today is also really good."

I give her a scarf I brought from Israel. She folds it around her neck, kisses me, and sends me with blessings to continue on my journey.

The lives of the women I met in India were influenced by their society's caste system and by their inferior status as women in the social hierarchy. Here, more than in any other place I visited, I felt the powerlessness of women and how much they had to put up with in the way they and their bodies are treated. That they must travel far from home to give birth, and have to obey the doctors and medical staff without question. The Dai Yogren of the Kullu Valley was also very angry about this. She doesn't think it is possible to change the status of women and perhaps isn't even interested in doing so. But as an elderly midwife, she feels deeply the pain of the changes and their effect on the women giving birth.

She weeps for the harm being caused to the bodies of women whom she knows personally. Along with this great sorrow, however, sometimes the pain of the loss of traditional ways is combined with happiness at the positive changes that technology has brought here. As Rimpal said from her perch in the Himalayas, once it was good and now it is also good. Once life was simple and the births would take place in familiar surroundings, but now some things in life are easier, the roads are open even in winter, and the medical opportunities are broader.

In India, birth is an extreme and crude expression of the accepted social standards of the population in all of its varied complexities and compartments. Hierarchy is clear-cut in all walks of life, profession, gender, age, and caste. Here, I was able to clearly see and understand the hierarchy that reigns at hospital births all over the world, beginning with government control. The regulations about birthing in India are unequivocal, and the government put its agenda in place by offering money to people who otherwise have none.

Throughout time and in many places, laws have been made by the ruling classes with the purpose of gaining control over the birth process – how births should take place, the number of births allowed, or encouraging more births. .

Already in Genesis, the first book of the Bible, God says to women that "in pain you will bring forth children. Your desire will be for your husband and he will rule over you." Good beginning. In Exodus, the Pharoah of Egypt commanded the Hebrew midwives to kill all the first-born males born to Jews. In China, laws were passed to limit the amount of births allowed per couple in order to prevent a population explosion. Many countries have laws about abortion. The control of reproduction of the species is a way of controlling citizens, and one of its main expressions is the decision that all births should take place in hospitals.

In India, having to give birth in hospital is very hard on women. They are already in a weak position in society and must now submit to further dominance over their lives. This is very detrimental to their well-being during labor and causes them great harm emotionally and physically.

In Israel, a law was passed to protect the rights of patients. It states, among other things, that it is the inalienable right of every person to choose what is done to his or her body according to his or her own beliefs and preferences. Every act that is done to a woman in labor, or to any other patient, must be agreed to by him or her. The idea is to give women in labor the possibility of acting in accordance with their own wishes and beliefs. The alternatives must be offered by law, together with an explanation of the dangers (risks) involved using this or that method.

The underlying problem is the way in which the options are expressed. It is not that the medical staff are trying to hide facts from women in labor, but the doctor himself is influenced by his own belief system, by his medical training, and by the protocols of his workplace. So even when he presents the alternatives to the birth mother, it tends to be in a biased manner because of his professional conditioning.

In many cases I have noted that the medical staff do not explain the whole picture. It is not malicious, but simply because their own experience and beliefs color their presentation. As someone who accompanies births in many different hospitals, I can recognize the different attitudes towards a 'normal, accepted' care of the woman in labor. Even the different shifts in a delivery room will include different medical teams at different times of the day and night, so that the delivery room experience will depend upon the team that is on call.

Often a woman in labor will have several changes of staff during her delivery. The possibilities she encounters will depend upon the staff member present, the type of room, the specific protocol of that hospital, and the personal experience and training of each staff member.

So what can be done?

We must first of all understand that regulation of births exists, and is driven by the worldview of birthing, by economics, and by accepted patriarchal views of the 'correct' birth process. I use the word patriarchal, because I am sorry to say that in Israel and other countries I see that the point of view of the medical hierarchy in the delivery room is not based only on professional diagnoses, but also on gender politics. Midwives with tens of years of experience must defer to decisions made by young doctors with very little experience.

Omi Leisner is a researcher at Bar-Ilan University. She has studied the changes put in place by the Israeli government and Health Department about birthing over the years. From the statistics she presents, it is possible to see how the position has changed according to political and economic factors. How rewards and punishments were used, and laws passed, which changed the rules according to the approach of the government in power at the time.

When the state was first established in 1948, most births took place at home with the help of midwives. The surrounding community would look after pregnant women both before and after the birth. The midwife and nurse would personally know each woman during her entire pregnancy, know her beliefs (religious or other) and respect her lifestyle. The state would pay for the midwife's services and would supply the necessary initial items for mother and baby.

For various reasons, including the rise in the status of doctors and a desire to 'modernize' the country's medical face, in addition to the economic interests of different political parties and interest groups, it was decided to move births to hospitals. Laws were immediately passed with the intention of getting women into hospitals and preventing home births as much as possible.

In a world without this control, a normal low-risk birth should take place at home (while always agreeing that a problem birth should be in a hospital under medical supervision). For some reason the Health Department in Israel changed its stance, stopped seeing pregnancy and birth as a natural and healthy process of life, and began to treat births as pathological. Since that time, and up until now, women's rights have been revoked (denied) and those women who decide to give birth at home are discouraged from doing so in many ways, even though they will have with them a certified midwife who carefully complies with the Health Department's requirements.

Thus, new controls were established. The cost of a home birth is paid for by the woman. It can amount to around $2000. The Health

Department does not cover this, even though twice that amount is allocated to a hospital for each birth there. Not only does the medical system impose strict regulations on women that have been devised and set in place by men, but the justice system also supports these decisions. The courts are usually ruled by male judges who approve these steps that take away from women their basic rights over their bodies, by means of legal arguments that have no relation to healthy birth practices.

Only recently a birthing center in Israel was closed on the pretext that it must be supervised by a higher authority and receive more authorizations, even though it was run by an experienced doctor and his staff and contained all the necessary modern medical equipment for birthing.

There is no doubt that a good medical system, professional and experienced, is very important, and this exists in Israel. But the need for a change in the hierarchy of the delivery room is just as important.

The rights of women to be able to choose must be restored. The amount of interference in a normal birth must be reduced, and control of the birth process left in the hands of the woman herself. The interventions where the doctor takes control can fatally harm the woman's health. Cesarean section is a complex and dangerous process, with possible detrimental long-term effects on a woman's health.

The view that the medical staff in a hospital are responsible for the safety of the unborn child contains the assumption that the parents are not responsible, and have agreed with that. Research by Omi Leisner in her book *Fertility Policies in Israel,* has demonstrated that most of the interference in births is not necessary, and takes place for hierarchical reasons that have no justifiable connection to the health of the woman and her baby.

I restate here my own view of birth, based on many years' experience, that it is a healthy and gentle traditional practice which can be beautiful at home or in a hospital. For example, in some hospitals midwives are now permitted to sew up tears in the perineum instead of having to call in a doctor. This is important, because if the new mother has received good care, warmth, and support from the midwife during the birth, she does not need to be exposed suddenly to a strange medical figure whom she does not know

Opinions about the hierarchy in delivery rooms and the reasons for passing laws that limit the freedom of choice for a woman in labor should be discussed openly, as well as the political, self-serving, and economic motives for decisions that are behind many of the changes in birthing policies. There should be an open dialogue between the woman in labor and the staff taking care of her, which takes into consideration the safety of the birth as well as the needs of the woman, and respects her rights over her own body and her autonomy. The discussion should take place in a deep and meaningful way, and include what is best for the birthing mother, for her baby to be, and the entire family.

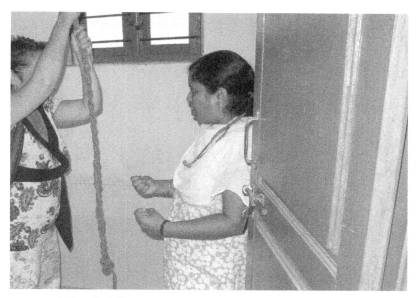

B.R Hills labor room in the jungle of Southern India

Dai Jera Maadama

Trance and fire for Durga, the Goddess of the new baby

Waiting for labor Dai Jera Maadama B.R. Hills

The entire family taking care of the baby on the train

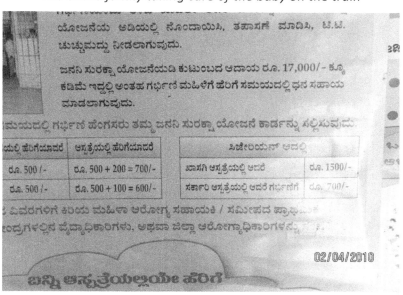

Incentives for hospital births- Karanatka Region

207

The Muslim Community

Everything is so dry. My lips are dry, my nose is dry. The sea glints to the west and Aqaba (the southernmost city in Jordan) slips away behind us as the car climbs the wide road. Big trucks carrying cargo from the port on the Red Sea into the arid desert country also climb the road. The sky is very blue and the iconic singer Umm Kulthum is singing on the radio.

"It is best to listen to Umm Kulthum in the middle of the night," says Eli, my taxi driver. His eyes are yellowish brown, like a tiger. He is from the Tafilah clan, which is based in the El-Tafilah region in Jordan. The mountains in the Tafilah region are high and soar over the Dana Valley. Towards the west you can see the hills of Jerusalem afar off.

When I met Latifah she was 110 years old, still fresh and clear-headed. Her only complaint was that she felt a bit cold and didn't see well because of a cataract. Latifah is a Hajja, meaning that she has been to Mecca one or more times. She is the local healer and midwife of this region. Today, a long line of people seeking her advice about their aches and pains of both body and soul, wait patiently.

Some people from Qatar love her so much that they are coming the following week to take her to hospital in Amman (the capital of Jordan) for a cataract operation

"They are paying for everything," her daughters tell me happily. Latifah herself never speaks about money and never asks for payment, but whoever comes to her for treatment pays generously at the end.

She is a small and wrinkled woman, who walks slowly around the simple room. She feels the gas cooker with her hands in order to know where to put the burning match and where to place the kettle on the fire. She digs around in the closet, looking for something, and when her daughter tries to help her, she scolds her to sit down, the tea will soon be ready.

The tea, when it comes, is sweet and warm.

Latifah sits close to me and looks into my eyes. I feel that she knows everything about me. She smiles and her wrinkled face wrinkles up even more. She places her hand on mine. It is large and speckled with age spots. Her fingers are long and the fingernails wide. I can feel the long fibers of the nails. Her skin is dry and her hand feels cool on mine

"In order to have a baby," she explains to me, "It is important that the woman be pure and that the husband and wife think about Allah. It is not enough to understand and accept the fact that God and the angels decide on the arrival of the baby into the world. At the time of intercourse, His name must be remembered in order to dispel Satan and the demons. Only Allah decides when that will happen, when the coupling will be successful. When He decides that it will happen, he sends messengers to guard over and assist the deed.

"The Angel Gabriel and the Angel Azriel stand ready for the

minute that the spark of life is ignited by Allah. The Angel Azriel is entrusted with the power of death, but he is a gentle angel, supportive and accepting. The Angel Gabriel is responsible for guarding the entrance to the womb, and creates the (character or image of) baby as God created the first man. Then and only then, if Allah decides that it really is the time to create a new person, when the husband enters into his wife, God creates the spirit of the new baby."

She looks up at the sky for a minute and says Al Hamdulilah (praise be to God).

"In order to protect the baby from demons and the evil eye, I pray and call the Prophet Noah by his name and ask him to separate this soul from all the other souls," she tells me. "This is important. The Prophet must be at hand because the minute the baby comes out Satan also arrives, and that is why the baby cries. "

She tells me how babies come into the world. God sends an angel to the fetus when he is 40 days old. This angel writes down the baby's life, how long it will be, what his character will be like, how he will make a living, exactly when and how he will die. God knows all mysteries beforehand. According to Islam, on the 40th day conception is complete and the fetus becomes a human being with a soul.

I have already heard about the formation of the baby in the presence of Allah. My wonderful friends Samira Mawassi and Rada Magdolin, from Al Qasami College in the town of Baqa al-Gharbiyye in Israel, told me about the Islamic belief in the transmigration of the soul until it becomes a baby. Samira and Rada both practice Naturopathy and work with pregnant women. They explained to me that every surah (chapter) in the Quran is divided into verses. A few chapters discuss the soul of man, pregnancy, and birth. In surah al-Fatiha, the first chapter, it is written that when a man understands that he comes from God, he will be humble during his lifetime. Man comes from Allah, Samira explained to me. In the Quran, seven stages are entailed, from the creation of the fetus until the baby's birth.

The first stage is 'dust' or 'ashes.' As the first man was created out of earth, so every new person created in the world is created from dust. During the second stage God mixes the ashes with water and forms clay. God creates the seed (sperm) which joins (is planted within) with the egg. Both sperm and the egg are made mostly of water, and therefore a human being is also mostly of water. Inside the seed and the egg are all the necessary plans for creating the fetus. The sperm is responsible for the gender of the newborn.

Now, as I sit with the old midwife – *daya* in Arabic – she places her right hand over her ear and begins to sing to me the surah which explains the stages of development of the fetus in the mother's womb. Between verses, she stops to translate for me and to make sure I understand what she is singing.

In the chapter it is written that after the seed enters the egg, the egg closes around it and the fetus is formed. Afterwards, the fetus turns into a piece of meat which has on it signs of being chewed. I think to myself that this must be the stage when the beginnings of the spinal column are seen. It does look like teeth marks.

I searched for a very long time to encounter traditional Muslim midwives or *dayas*. It was not easy to find these women. I asked everyone I could. I looked for women who were not midwives, but who still remembered what had been done to them by traditional midwives. I asked them to teach me whatever they knew about beliefs, theories, ancient writings, and practical methods that were used during pregnancy and birth.

"Hajja Latifah," I say, "I have heard that when the baby is born, his father sings Allahu akbar (God is great) into his right ear."

She holds my face between her two large hands, smiles a wrinkly smile and kisses my ear. I hear an explosion. Next she glues her mouth to my ear, her hand is on my shoulder and begins to sing Aaaalllllahu Aakbar right into my ear. Chills run through my entire body. The hot air moves from her ancient mouth straight into my brain. The pounding of my heart gets stronger.

She keeps going, and I feel the sounds penetrating into every membrane and cell in my body. The vibrations tingle up and down my spine. My eyes fill with tears and I start to cry. She holds me up as I almost fall; she hugs me tight as I sob inside her hug. She holds my face and I see up close the geometric tattoos on her forehead, cheek, and around her eyes. The curlicues made so long ago to ornament and mark her.

She kisses me on the mouth, her lips are soft. She laughs and says, "That's what they do to the baby after his birth, so that he will be healthy and whole."

"The father of the baby does this?"

"No," says Latifah. "I do that. That is my job. The father is not present at the birth, he is not allowed. It is important that the baby hears it immediately, the minute he is born. Afterwards the father will also do it. In this way faith enters his body and Allah will protect him."

Hamida, Latifah's daughter, is wrapped in a burka and only her green eyes peek out. They are expressive eyes and she tells me she has nine boys and seven girls. I ask her about the deliveries. She tells me about one night when she was visiting relatives in a different village, "Suddenly I felt that I was about to give birth. My mother could not make it in time and neither could the village midwife where I was. I delivered before she arrived."

"So how was the birth?" I ask.

"Allah was with me."

I am dumbstruck. "What, nobody was with you? You were alone?"

"No." She is surprised at my question. "Of course I was not alone, the neighborhood women came to help me."

Latifa tells me that ever since she was three years old her mother took her with her to birthings. She laughs, "I was always a *daya*! I learned from what I saw. That's how all the midwives are. We all learned from our mothers and from experience. Sometimes they would come to call me at night. Usually the husband would come. I would always go, never mind the weather.

"Sometimes the birth would be so fast, I wouldn't manage to get there in time. But there was nothing to worry about. Allah is always there, and there is always a mother or another woman that knows what to do. Even if a woman gives birth in a field, there will always be other women from the village who have already given birth and know what to do.

"A midwife is needed. It is forbidden for an impure woman to be at the birth, because the birth must be pure. If an impure woman is in the room, the birth will be long, or – God forbid – the woman will not be able to conceive again."

Latifah nods her head gravely. "That can cause the baby to be born sickly, or a pest or maybe he will have scabies. When I assist at births I tell the women that they must pray, because the angels are going up and down and see everything that goes on here. I remind them of the seriousness of this moment. Remind them that the woman in labor is in God's hands. She is in transition between heaven and earth, between life and death. She is on the edge of a great abyss, the edge of a precipice."

The meaning of the word pit in Hebrew is abyss and also womb.

"The birth experience is very similar to the death experience," says Latifah. "I ask the women to bring stones and soil to the delivery room so that there will be a connection to nature and to the earth, but also because the earth and stones are like a hole in the ground."

I am reminded of thoughts I had about birth and death when I returned from The Gambia.

Can the mother of the woman in childbirth be at the birth, I ask. Latifah says that sometimes it is good and sometimes not good. There is one prayer that says that if Allah wants to, he will help with the birth, but he cannot if her mother is there.

Fatima, another of Latifah's daughters, sits with us. She says that sometimes it puts pressure on the daughter if the mother is present, but in other instances a woman will go to her mother to have the baby. Latifah adds that a woman in the middle of her pregnancy should not be present at a birth, because when she hears the screams, her baby will get scared and not want to come out, or might come out too early.

Latifah is a very pious woman and prays five times a day, as is required of Muslims. I ask her if she prays in the delivery room if it is the time for prayer. "No," she answers. "It is forbidden for women to pray if they have their period and also at a birth. There are a lot of secretions and it is not good to pray to Allah in dirty conditions.

"A woman is not allowed to say the chapters of the Quran, but she will say 'Allah be with me, Allah do not desert me,' over and over again." She shows me how the woman raises her hands to the sky and pleads with God.

During the painful phase of the birth, the woman in labor and the angels are able to go up and down between heaven and earth. The gates of heaven are open at this time and all the people present can send wishes up to God. For example, it is customary to ask that travelers will return safely, that the sick will get well, for Allah to open the eyes of the blind, to enrich the poor, to free prisoners, and to protect us from bad government.

Latifah then says in a low voice, "We also have to get rid of the demons present and this is done by repetition of certain prayers. 'In the name of Allah the generous and merciful, and in the name of the goddess who watches over mothers and the babies.' But it is forbidden to talk about this too much," she adds. "It is forbidden to bring up the name of the female childbed demon Qarinah, because if you say it, she immediately comes and starts to make trouble."

Another daughter joins us. Her name is Meha and she also is wrapped in a burka with only her dark eyes showing. "When I gave birth I screamed a lot," she says. "I screamed on purpose. Allah wants us to beg him to be with us. We all know that it is important to scream during the birth. If the birth is difficult, there is even a special prayer that describes Allah in a blue tent because Allah lives in heaven in a blue tent."

We sit on mattresses on the floor. A heater is lit in the small room even though it is hot outside. In the corner stands a bed covered by colorful blankets. Latifah has me lie on the bed in order to show me how she turns a baby inside the mother's stomach. She explains to me that at one time a breech baby could lead to severe complications during deliveries and even cause death to the mother. She places her hands on my stomach, waits, and then she starts to move them very slowly.

"I show the baby where to go," she says. "It must be done very slowly and very gently. He already knows the way if he chooses to go. If he stays with his head up, maybe the mother will die, but maybe not. Everything is from Allah."

The hands of elderly midwives always take me by surprise. Usually

I do not like massages because they are never accurate enough, but these hands have something special. The touch is exactly in the right place, it comforts me and gives me confidence.

The feeling of love that enters me from her hands reminds me of the touches of all the wise women I have met in my travels, The midwives of Madagascar who showed me how they massage the birthing mother and turn the baby, the grandmothers who hugged me and into whose hugs I could completely relax, and now these wonderful hands.

Freshly baked pita bread is served with olive oil pressed from this summer's olives, and za'atar (a Middle Eastern spice mixture of oregano and other herbs) picked locally in the hills of Tafilah. The pita fills me with happiness. After we eat, we talk about life in general, and then I must leave. At the end of the winter the news reaches me that Hajja Latifah has died. My heart contracts and I feel that someone important has gone from this world. Something from the past is gone and will never be here again. The village of Kfar Salam is located near the Arab city of Nablus, known as Shechem in Hebrew, in the West Bank or Palestinian Territories about an hour's drive from my home in Israel. It's a pleasant drive. The road is wide and has a view of the Shomron (Samarian) hills in the dryness of late summer. A few tall squills growing by the side of the road show that autumn is near.

Abdallah is waiting for me on the Palestinian side of the border checkpoint between Israel and the Palestinian Territories and asks that I let him drive the car. He doesn't want his friends from the village to see a woman driving him. I move over to the passenger seat. He is a terrible driver. I had been told that the drive to the West Bank would be dangerous and that I would be afraid, but up until now I was fine. The road has sharp curves and trucks blow their horns with impatience. Abdallah is not very careful and I am shaking and sweating with fear.

The smell of smoke rises to my nostrils as we drive through the alleyways of the village. We turn right toward the hills, and the road becomes even more treacherous. Around us are herds of sheep, goats, and donkeys. We veer around another curve, one more steep incline, and arrive at a large orchard. Olive, fig, lemon, pomegranate, avocado and grapefruit trees and grape vines. On the roofs of the houses around the orchard are black water storage tanks.

I get out of the car, fastening another button on my long-sleeved shirt that I wore over my dress for modesty. I am a little excited and also feeling shy. Children come skipping from all corners, speaking very fast in Arabic. From the porch peeks a figure wrapped in cloth from head to toe.

"Salaam Aleikum (peace be upon you)," I say and an excited chorus of voices returns my greeting.

Ayat, the wife of Abdallah, hugs me and kisses me on each cheek. She holds my hand in both of her hands and smiles broadly. "Tfaadali, tfaadali, welcome welcome."

I am invited into the house. I understand very little Arabic, but the smiling eyes of Ayat tell me a lot. Abdullah translates a few words after I look at him and ask for his help. Abdallah and I have been speaking for years together about our homes, our lives, how it is here, how it is there. Each of us from our own point of view. Abdallah works very hard to support his family. In order to put food on his family's table he stays away all week working in Israel, so that his children will be well educated.

Since my work deals with pregnancy, birth, and young children, I was kept up to date about his wife's last pregnancy and about the tragedy that happened.

The house is well kept and sparkling clean. The living room is full of big sofas, pillows, dried flowers, colorful curtains, and pictures of the Al Aqsa Mosque in Jerusalem and verses from the Quran. There are also photos of women of all ages. They look rather alike, and are Abdallah's sisters, cousins, and aunts.

Almost all wear traditional attire – a long dark dress with embroidery, and over it a coat that reaches the floor, with buttons up to the neck, and a scarf that covers the head and neck. Two young women, Abdallah's daughter and a niece of Ayat, are wearing tight jeans with a traditional head covering (hijab).

Abdallah has organized a meeting for me with a local midwife. Her name is Basita ('simple' in English). She already waits for me. Her eyes are shining and she has a colorful dress and white head-scarf. Like most of the women in the village, *daya* Basita does not speak Hebrew. For years now the women have not come into Israel. This discussion is in Arabic, with Abdallah translating into Hebrew and vice versa.

"What do you mean – how are the births? We have babies, no?" She looks at me and doesn't understand what I am asking. Shamas, one of the young women in jeans and head scarf, who studies Islam at university, says, "Everything is in the Quran, in the chapter about the delivery of Mariam, there all the secrets of giving birth are written."

She is talking about Mary giving birth to Jesus. The Quran has stories from both the Old and New Testaments. She sings me the verses and explains them. The women of Abdallah's family sit silently with us. Samira and Rada had also explained to me the verses about Mary which contain all the ingredients for a good birth to occur. Once again I find myself listening to the melody and the words.

"So she conceived him and she withdrew with him to a remote place. And the pains of childbirth drove her to the trunk of a date palm tree. She said, 'Oh I wish I had died before this and was in oblivion, forgotten.' But a voice called from below her, 'Do not grieve, your Lord has provided beneath you a stream. Shake thyself toward the trunk of the date palm. It will drop upon you fresh dates. So eat and drink and be content. Keep working normally, be in peace with God and with yourself. If thou see any man say, 'I have vowed a fast to God and this day I will not talk with any human being.'"

In this chapter Mary asks for help. She is in distress because of her situation and also because her contractions are strong. She is in a remote place in the desert under the shade of a date palm. She is naturally drawn to a warm place because the oxytocin secreted during the contractions needs warmth in order to secrete properly. She turns to Allah in despair and asks for comfort, and cries out that she wants to die. Nearly every woman in labor feels desperate when she is nearly fully dilated. At that point the oxytocin and adrenalin hormones are at their highest level. This is when the woman feels as if she is going to die, and in a way she does. The woman that she was up to this moment will not exist anymore.

Mary knows that the baby is coming down from the spiritual plane into the earthly realm. She feels she is at a place and time between the two worlds. The verses may also refer to the specter of death, which is present at all births.

The Angel guides Mary and encourages her to continue to believe in God, who will help her. To trust in the powers that guide and assist with the birth, which are critical at every birth.

The angel draws Mary's attention to the stream that Allah has placed at her feet. It is well known that one way to assuage the pain of childbirth is to be immersed in water. Births in water are gentle and reduce the risk of tearing the perineum. To drink water is also important, so the fact that there is a source of water provided by God is relevant.

The angel continues to encourage the woman in labor and to give her what she needs to deliver a healthy baby. He instructs her to shake the palm tree, which will cause her to move her body as well as receive nourishment. The movements that are helpful in labor are those where the woman is in a vertical position, because gravity helps the baby move down into the correct position in the pelvis. Movements of the pelvis and the whole body help to relieve pain during the birth.

It is difficult to shake a palm tree, but if you lean on it with your hands raised and try to move it, this position will create movement of your whole body. As in many cultures – for example the hanging sari in the hut in the jungle – the woman holds something higher than herself. These movements raise her rib cage and create space for the uterus to be able to do its work at maximum potential.

The angel urges Mary to eat the dates that fall from the tree. Samira and Rada told me that it is a tradition of Arab women to eat dates during the last month of pregnancy. Scientific research at the University of Jordan showed that eating Medjool dates shortens the duration of active labor significantly. One group of pregnant women ate six Medjool dates every day for their last four weeks of pregnancy. The control group ate no dates. The delivery time of the group who ate dates was shorter and required less intervention. Samira and Rada had told me that Medjool dates contain a substance similar to oxytocin, which affects contractions during labor.

The angel tells Mary to be at peace and get rid of anyone who disturbs her. He advises her to tell them that she has taken a vow of silence and cannot answer them.

This recipe for the ultimate birth experience thrills me no end. All the physiological and spiritual wisdom needed for a safe and healthy birth is contained in this one chapter. The belief in a higher power, the description of the spiritual situation of a woman going through a significant life change, advice about optimal physical movement and the best position for the birth, advice to be silent and go inside oneself, the use of water, the use of heat, the oxytocin added with the dates – all the most important knowledge is written in these few verses.

I ask the elderly *daya* what she gives to women to ease their pregnancy or labor. She sends a girl to the kitchen to prepare *kirpa*. A steaming cup is served to me.

"Ahh, cinnamon," I say.

"Yes," she says, "it is important to heat the woman and cinnamon tea is good for that."

Throughout my travels I met with midwives from different cultures, and each one I interviewed told me of a food or drink with warming properties that they give to the woman during or after labor.

In Peru, midwives prepare a tea with duck feathers and mustard seed. (The feathers are covered in grease Boiling them will give the woman in labor energy from the fat, and heat from the infusion of the mustard seeds). In Ethiopia, midwives make a dish which contains *samna* (clarified butter), ginger, black pepper and other hot spices. In Madagascar, the woman is given very hot water to drink and eats rice with gingery soup. The midwife from Mexico, Naoli Vinaver, prepares a brew containing black pepper, cloves, ginger, cinnamon, bay leaf and a branch from an avocado tree! Into theh boiling water with all the flavors she mixes a generous quantity of 90% cocoa. It tastes like very spicy chocolate. In Alaska they give whale blubber, and in India black cumin seed, and massage with apricot oil. The Moroccan grandmothers bring an omelet made with cumin to the house of the new mother and serve this *kirpa*, the same strong cinnamon tea used by the Muslim women here.

I always asked the midwives why they give these energy foods filled with fats, proteins, and heat, and they reply that that is what their mothers taught them. They do not know that heat stimulates the oxytocin to secrete and helps the birth to progress, but they know very well all the secrets to encourage labor.

The children here in Salam village serve us refreshments of pretzels, cookies, dates, and juice. Ayat sits a little to the side. She is smiling but her eyes are sad. I can see that something is bothering her. Abdallah sees my look and says that Aya's back hurts her, and she is pregnant again.

Ayat says, "The doctors in the hospital are good. I believe God will help me and this time everything will be fine." I look at her. Her eyes are filled with tears. She gets up, goes over to the closet and brings out a picture of a sweet baby. We both look at him in silence. This last baby died when he was still very young.

"He was sick," Abdallah told me. "We took him to the hospital and they said everything was fine. We took him back home but he still did not feel well. We returned again to the hospital and he died."

Ayat says it is not good to prepare things for the baby in advance. She talks about what can be done to protect the baby from demons and the evil eye. One of them is a "shirt of salt." A shirt of salt is like a layer of protection for the baby, such as washing him after the birth, and not preparing anything before the birth. The idea is to prevent the demoness Qarinah from knowing that a baby is on the way. In order to preserve the baby's luck, flour should be taken from seven houses, and pitas baked on an iron surface and placed on the baby. They must then be given to a black dog to eat. Alternatively, water can be taken from seven wells, put out under the stars for seven nights, and then used to bathe the baby in water that has not seen the sun.

We all look at the photograph. Ayat sighs. "My back hurts a lot," she says.

"Mine too," says Fatma, a younger sister who is supposed to give birth a few weeks before Ayat. "I cannot sleep at night."

Basita invites Ayat to come and sit beside her. She places her warm hands on the young woman's back and massages her with slow movements. Ayat sighs gratefully, "That's good."

The *daya* invites me too and demonstrates the massage. "More," I say, "More. It is so good, why does one have to be pregnant to feel these hands?"

Everyone laughs. Without hesitation I lie down on the floor. The surprised looks don't bother me. The children giggle. "Come Ayat, you too, and you too, Fatma. Your back hurts – do yoga."

All the men move into the next room and the women lie down on the rug. Together we do some yoga positions that relieve back pain. The elderly *daya* Basita sits on the couch and watches us knowingly.

Food is served at the table. I am offered stuffed grape leaves, spicy stew, fragrant rice, hummus, hot peppers, and tomato and onion salad in olive oil. Everything tastes amazing. The food here is so simple and fresh. The flour is freshly ground, bread just baked, vegetables straight from the fields, olives from their orchard, and milk straight from the udder.

Ayat wants me to tell her about the birth of my granddaughter in America. I tell her that it was a home birth and was very quick and wonderful. A midwife was present and another assistant midwife, and I was also there.

"What? You didn't make it to the hospital? Why was the midwife at the house?"

"No," I say, "my daughter chose to give birth at home."

"Why? Aren't the hospitals in America good? Are the doctors not good?" Shams, their daughter, opens her green eyes wide.

"They are excellent," I reply.

"So your daughter is a bit primitive? Old-fashioned?"

I laugh and say that my daughter Dana is actually a very modern woman, but she believed that her body knows how to give birth and she only needed a good midwife to be there. If some complication occurred, they would all go to the hospital delivery room. Basita sits and smiles while one of the women translates for her.

"So your daughter trusts in God," she says. I nod with a smile.

Latifah, the Hajja from Tafilah, Basita and all the other older Muslim women I spoke with said that most of the births in their villages are short. There were instances where the woman went out to work in the fields, squatted to give birth, and returned home with the new baby.

"Birth is a part of life," said Hajja Laifah. "Most of the births last a maximum of two hours. The pains are barely felt, the contractions slip in and out like thieves in the night. When the women can no longer lie down or sit, that is the sign that the birth is very close at hand. We have an expression for this – 'like sitting on a pile of rocks.' Or when we see clouds piling up in the sky, we say they are like pregnant women getting ready to give birth any minute."

When traditional midwives from all over the world spoke to me about short delivery times I had at first assumed that they were referring to the second phase of labor, when the contractions are strong and urge the mother to push, and the baby emerges. I thought that they were not including the latent phase when the contractions have just begun. Little by little I began to realize that they meant the entire period of labor. Some births do take longer, but the normal length of a birth in traditional societies is much, much shorter than in modern societies.

I ask Basita if she does an internal exam to fathom how the birth is progressing. Does she check how big the opening of the cervix is? She tells me that usually this is not necessary. Only when she thinks the birth will take a long time will she check to make sure the baby is well.

"Usually I just know when the time is near. There are signs, for example – if the woman's legs are shaking or she begins to sweat."

I know these signs. I have also noticed the changes in behavior of the woman who goes through natural labor when there is no medical intervention. She will make sounds and her heels will rise up during each contraction as she leans against something. Or she will suddenly feel very warm and begin to sweat. All these are signs that the baby will be coming very soon.

"Which position do you think is the best for the birth?" I ask Basita.

"When two women stand behind the woman in labor just before the baby emerges and she leans on them. They sway with her as if to shake the baby out. When I see the top of the baby's crown, I just put out my two hands to catch him so that he won't touch the floor."

"What do you do about the placenta? Do you help it to come out?"

"If the placenta is reluctant to come out, I give the mother olive oil to drink and put my finger down her throat so that she will vomit. The action of vomiting helps to separate the placenta. I place the afterbirth next to the baby so that he can receive nourishment from it. So he can drink the blood from it for at least 12 hours.

I asked the same question of Umm Hani, a midwife from Kalkilya, another Israeli Muslim village, and she answered that when the placenta is lingering she ties a string to the umbilical cord and to the big toe of the mother so that when she feels contractions she will pull out the afterbirth. Or she lets her breathe into a bottle.

Basita tells me about her daily life and about her daughters, who are used to hard physical labor every day. They pick the olives, take care of the goats, grow vegetables, take care of the house and the children. I think of the women I met in Dakota, in Alaska, in Madagascar. Hard physical labor makes their bodies flexible, their muscles and tendons strong. Years of crouching, squatting, bending, lifting and carrying loads has made them fit for giving birth to a baby. A woman who works during her daily life knows how to work during her delivery.

"If I was able to walk from Jericho to Shechem-Nablus with a donkey with no problem, and if I am able to carry a sack of 12 kilos on my head for hours on end, why should it be a problem to have a baby?" asks Basita.

In any case, even though Basita describes short birth times, she does not completely deny labor pains and does not describe birth as easy as fruit falling from a tree. Her understanding of the pain is that it hurts because of the punishment from the Garden of Eden. When a woman screams during labor it is also because of the hardships she will face to raise those children, and because it is not easy to remain faithful to God.

"It is good to shout during the birth. Suffering is what was promised to us in the Garden of Eden and we must remember to call to Allah to help us." Everyone nods in agreement with this.

Basita tells me how she takes care of the mother after the birth. First, the mother must get coffee without sugar and must rest, even if her house is still full of the women who came to help. Usually her mother will be the one taking care of her.

"In the olden days we would wrap up the body of the new mother so that her body would be compressed and she would not bulge out. This would also help control her shaking after the birth. We would touch and work on her because the bones move, and we put them back in place. We would massage her from bottom to top to restore her health. Today we give chicken soup. From a rooster if she had a girl baby and from a hen if she had a boy. Symbolizing their finding of a mate in the future."

"The new mother receives special foods," she says, as they serve me a steaming dish. My mouth fills with its good taste and scent, and it is warm and comforting. This dish is called *shidha*, which means strength in Arabic. It is also called 'forty' because it has 40 ingredients and the woman should eat this for 40 days after the birth. It contains orange lentils, carrots, black-eyed peas, cauliflower, grape leaves, spinach, potatoes and peppers, milk products, shellfish, rabbit meat and much more.

I imagine how a traditional birth would be here. A young woman in her home, surrounded by neighbors, sisters and perhaps a *daya*. I imagine that Basita from Shechem or Latifah is present, or another woman dressed in traditional attire with her head covered and her hands warm. They are making sweet cinnamon *kirpa* tea for the woman in labor. The woman is sitting bent over, or is swaying and moving around the room. The women place warm stones on her lower back to ease her pains. They encourage her, while preparing what is needed for the new baby.

During my search for material dealing with pregnancy and birth in traditional Muslim society, I came across a book by Hilma Granqvist in the basement of the University of Tel Aviv. Its pages were yellowing and its cover smelt of days long gone. Hilma was a Finnish/Swedish anthropologist born in 1890 who wanted to investigate how children grew up in biblical times. She came to what was then British Palestine in 1925 and wandered around Jerusalem and Bethlehem, finally settling in a village called Artas. She spoke with women who were working the land and assumed that their way of life reflected the customs and traditions of the ancient tribes of Israel.

When I read through the pages of her book, I was able to feel the sweetness of the warm sun and hear the women's voices chattering about their daily lives while working in the fields. Hilma stayed a long time in the village of Artas. I cringed when I read her description of women whose babies were aborted as a result of hard work or family violence.

She wrote that it was forbidden for a woman to work too hard or carry heavy loads while pregnant. If she did work, and her fetus spontaneously aborted, someone from her family would have to pay 'blood money.' The baby belongs to the father, even while still in his mother's womb, and the woman and her family are held responsible for the death. On the other hand, if a man beat his wife and the baby died as a consequence, no complaint would be brought against him because the baby was his property.

Hilma wrote that the *daya* in the Muslim societies she researched were always older women. Women with experience, charisma, and well-respected in the community. Everyone would do as she told them and trusted her completely. When a midwife entered the room, she brought with her an atmosphere of tranquility and dignity. She was able to prevent the women from fighting, complaining, and cursing. Hilma added that local midwives told her how important a calm atmosphere is during childbirth. If the labor was long and the woman was becoming nervous, they would place prayer beads from Mecca around her neck. This would work like a medication and calm her.

In order to make the atmosphere holy, some midwives would burn a blue prayer rug inside the room. The rug symbolizes God's heavenly abode. I asked Basita about this. She had heard of the custom and agreed that the smoke would have a good effect.

"It would always calm the woman in labor," she told me. "Once I gave the order to make smoke, and the mother tried to light it but her hands were too shaky. I let someone else light the rug, and then I put out the fire and let the woman in labor inhale the smoke. Immediately afterwards the baby came out. The coughing and sneezing from the smoke can also be used to make the afterbirth come out quickly.

Hilma writes that the women of Artas and Shechem called the placenta 'the sister' and if she would be reluctant to come out they would call and talk to her, "Come out sister, your brother is waiting for you."

The Arab women explained to Hilma that the moment the umbilical cord is cut is the moment when the Gates of Heaven are open. . This is the time for supplications and requests to Allah. The timing is very important, they told Hilma. The time of the cutting of the cord has meaning and must be done carefully in exactly the right manner. Just as you do not eat in summer what was grown during winter. In the same way, you do not sever at night what you should sever in the day. Just as you don't harvest hay in the dark or pick fruit at night, that's how it is with the umbilical cord; you don't cut it at night, you wait until morning.

The women I interviewed in Arab communities told me that if the baby comes out in the evening, the umbilical cord will not be cut at night. They will wait until morning. And if he's born in the morning they will cut it in the late afternoon.

In Western cultures there are also women who observe the custom of waiting to cut the umbilical cord until it stops beating, and some wait until the placenta comes out before cutting the cord. A few women leave the placenta attached to the baby until the cord completely dries up and falls off on its own. This is called a lotus birth, and if the surroundings are kept very clean there is no danger from this procedure. The waiting time allows the placental blood to flow into the baby's body.

There are contrary views that too much blood flowing to the baby causes an overload to his liver and increases the likelihood of jaundice.

Hilma heard that the afterbirth is buried deep underground, and Basita affirmed that it is especially important to dig deep so that it will not be eaten by an animal. This could harm the woman's future chances of pregnancy.

Hilma wrote that the women would tie a string to the cord and place a bandage containing salt mixed with olive oil over the navel to dry it out. The remains of the navel they would rub into the middle of the baby's forehead to ensure good vision. They would then take this little piece and place it in his pillow to confuse the demoness Qarinah, the enemy of mothers and babies. The afterbirth would be hung in the doorway of the house (after it has been cleaned with salt) to keep Qarinah away.

Using salt as a protective and sterilizing agent is a constant theme among traditional cultures. The baby is often massaged with ointment that has salt in it, even over his eyes. The rinazaza of Madagascar combined salt with their herbs as a disinfectant when they massage the baby. The Druze women in the high mountains in the north of Israel, and in Syria, wash the baby in salt water, and if a child behaves badly they put salt on his head so he will return to his good behavior.

Majdal Shams is a Druze village in the mountains of northern Israel. I traveled there to meet with a group of older women. I was to teach these mothers how they can support their daughters during their childbirth in hospitals. When I arrived it was raining, and the entire village was enclosed in fog. We sat together in a heated room with cups of tea, and spoke about life today and how things have changed. On a large metal tray there were nuts, olives, and tiny eggplants pickled in olive oil and spices.

The Druze are not Muslims and do not believe in Allah, but in various prophets. Details of their religion are kept secret to this day.

The women told me that the last *daya* of their village had died the previous winter, aged 108. The *dayas* would still perform home births even when women began going to hospital. There were always women who gave birth at home, especially when the snow was high and travel became difficult.

When we spoke about births in olden times the eldest grand-mother showed me how it was done. She sat on the floor with her legs apart and had me sit between them with my back leaning on her stomach. She held me with both arms under my armpits and one woman sat in front of us to catch the baby. We laughed as we performed the show, but they explained in all seriousness that there was always someone sitting behind the birthing mother.

They told me that they would calm the woman in labor with warm words and tell her about the new soul that was about to enter her baby. It would be the soul of some family member who had died not long ago. According to their beliefs it is important that that soul returns to the world.

Fahima learned how to massage babies from her mother, and I have come to the Arab village of Kfar Kasem in central Israel to see how she does it. We sit in her living room, which is full of heavy furniture, pictures of the Al-Aksa mosque in Jerusalem, and surahs from the Quran.

At the entrance to the house a large room is filled with square ovens of sizzling coals. Fahima supports her family by baking because her husband is ill. When I arrive I find her kneading dough that she will bake over the hot coals to make pita. She sells it to restaurants in the area. Come eat, she says, we will talk after. She serves me fresh hot pita with a dip of grated tomatoes on the side, along with bowls of homemade olives and olive oil spiced with sesame and oregano. Her daughters and daughters-in-law join us.

After the meal she undresses her four-month-old grandson to demonstrate how she massages. She sits on a low wooden stool with her legs stretched in front of her and the baby placed on her legs. She coats her hands with olive oil and begins the massage. It is similar to what I saw done in The Gambia. At first, she just spreads the oil all over the baby's skin, moving her hands over his stomach, arms, legs and head.

Her touch deepens at his shoulders, and down the length of his arms and palms of his hands. She deeply massages his thigh joints and down his legs. A gentler touch for his stomach, chest, and mouth. She then crosses his arms and legs to the front and turns him over. She now uses her fingers on each side of his spinal column.

The midwife or the mother must do this massage for the first seven days with olive oil and salt. This protects the baby and influences his character. If this is not done correctly the child will be naughty. She laughs as she says that if a child is naughty we say to him, "Shame on you, put salt in your eyes." The women of Majdal

Shams had also told me about the custom of washing the baby in olive oil with salt to prevent infections.

"If the baby's head is not shaped nicely," Fahima explains to me while she massages the baby, "the midwife takes long strips of cloth and ties them around his head, like you do to people with headaches." She demonstrates by taking a triangle of cloth and wrapping it tightly around the baby's head. He looks like a miniature mummy.

"All babies here are cared for in this way. Now and always. The mother would do this or the grandmother. I saw how my mother took care of my older children and I decided to care for my younger children in the same way. Today, the young women want me to take care of their babies."

As I drive home I promise myself that I will continue to search for Muslim midwives to learn from while they are still here. I want to catch their last words of wisdom. The *daya* Latifah had died, Basita is no longer young, all the Druze midwives have died. In the Sinai Peninsula there are still a few women who practice midwifery in the hills. I feel that time is running out. The old *dayas* speak of natural childbirth as quick, shrouded in the mystery of Allah, and aided and protected by Him. Allah is the creator and the destroyer and everything that happens is blessed, whether good or bad. Faith is the main factor in all of their descriptions of childbirth.

The knowledge of how to give birth exists in a woman's body or is given to her by an agent of God, depending on one's point of view. All the Muslim women mention that they pray during delivery.

In each of the traditional societies that I visited, especially the ones where people live in accordance with nature, the relation to God is simple and direct. The belief that all is in His hands is deeply embedded in these people, even when the outcome is difficult to bear. The *yorgen* in Northern India, the Tibetan midwives, Jerra

Ma'adama from the jungles of southern Bangalore, and all the women I spoke to always said, "What will be will be."

In the Muslim community, trust in God is very strong. In the surah about Marie, this ingredient is vital to the story. God is here, by your side, don't be afraid. He has given you a stream of water to help you. He is here. Even if you fear for your life, trust in Allah.

In Judaism, childbirth is considered to be the life experience that brings one closest to God. This is the time when Heaven and Earth are connected.

It would seem that to wise grandmothers the existence of angels is beyond any shadow of a doubt. Midwives all over the world pray and ask for help from whatever powers they believe in. The belief in God and belief in the capabilities of the body go hand in hand.

Just as the heart beats, the digestive system works and the eyes see – all of man's bodily systems function without need of intervention. In the same way, giving birth to a baby just occurs, there is no need to DO anything, just let things happen on their own. During birth, the uterus begins its contractions, the cervical canal opens, the baby makes his way down through his mother's pelvis, which is perfectly suited to this job, and is pushed out into the air. The hormones that awaken the contractions of the uterus include oxytocin, endorphins and many others serve to regulate the tempo of this dance.

Ina May Gaskin, the famous home midwife who taught other midwives during the 1960s and up until today in the United States, speaks about the importance of prayers and faith in a midwife's work. According to her, a midwife must realize that the birth is a sacred event and that she, the midwife, is doing divine work. She should be aware that during the birth process, exceptional forces are at work, both physical and magical. Ina May directs women during their pregnancy to become aware every day of the miracle of birth and its spirituality.

Michel Odent, the influential French obstetrician, adds that prayer can be useful physiologically as well. He explains that prayer helps women to concentrate on their inner being, which assists in maximizing hormonal action during labor. It helps to remove brain function from the 'logical' part of the brain, allowing the woman to enter into a different place in space and time. Dr. Odent says that the secret to a good birth is to leave the woman alone. Just don't bother her. Trust in her ability to give birth and help her to believe in her body's ability and her power as a woman.

He explains that when the woman in labor crouches on her knees, as Christians and Moslems do when they pray, this position helps her to cut herself off from the outside world and enter inside herself. He says that this posture weakens the activity of the neocortex, which will serve to increase the hormonal secretions that in turn assist the useful contractions of the uterus and reduce the pain of these contractions. The position also allows the baby to comfortably enter into the pelvis.

I have found that the women of today have lost their trust and belief in their own ability to give birth. This is mostly because the male medical system has taken control of the process and convinced women not to 'suffer' during labor, but it is also partly because modern life has weakened their ability to withstand pain and cope with the emotional turmoil of birthing.

Sayings such as "Why suffer" and "Don't be old-fashioned," or "It's primitive to give birth without pain relievers" are phrases I hear over and over again in delivery rooms.

Young women I met in the Sinai desert, and women from large cities in Egypt, Bedouin women from towns and villages, are all delivering their babies by Cesarean section. They explain to me that they are afraid to have an epidural or other pain-killing drugs and the doctors advise them to have a Cesarean. Even their strong belief in Allah doesn't help them when facing doctors in hospitals.

In Israel, too, the system has destroyed women's faith in their own ability to give birth. The incidence of Cesareans performed is much lower than in Egypt or other Third World countries, solely because here it is possible to receive other forms of pain relief.

The number of women in the modern world who trust in their own ability to cope with the pain and experience of natural child-birth is very small. How can we reestablish in women the faith they once had in their own bodies and abilities?

During my work in delivery rooms I see very clearly how simple and possible it is to achieve this goal. All that is needed is a midwife who respects the needs and wishes of the birthing mother. One with patience to explain the process, who can encourage, comfort, and empower the woman in labor. Who has faith in the ability of the woman and the baby.

A midwife like this can greatly influence what takes place in the delivery room. Staff members who support the woman in her decisions, as well as the support of her partner or mother, or whoever is there, can completely turn around the experience. A doula who accompanies the birthing mother and backs her up in her decisions from the beginning can help to create this space of trust.

Research has shown that when another woman is present at the birth whose aim is to support the woman in labor and ease her pain with natural techniques, the results are very greatly improved. The birth will require less medical intervention, fewer Cesarean sections will be performed, fewer births will require the use of instruments, and less harm will come to babies and mothers. Along with these benefits, there will be a significant rise in the satisfaction of the mother with her birth experience.

The mother-to-be should be able to create for herself the kind of birth that is right for her. If she hears stories of births that actually happened and which empower women, they will strengthen her faith in her ability. If she trusts in nature to do at the birth what it does every day – to control bodily functions – she will be giving herself the best chances of having a happy and healthy delivery.

St Katrina Village Sinai Egypt

Daya Midwife Amar in Sinai Desert Egypt

Practicing Labor with Midwife Samira in Mountain Village

Sinai Desert

Midwife Latifa

Midwife Latifa and I

Conclusion

My research into traditional midwives and my work as a doula in the Western world have shown me that while progress in the medical field has increased safety and control during the birthing process, important elements have been lost.

Ancient ways acquired through centuries of experience and passed down from generation to generation are disappearing.

The natural process of creating a new life is now considered to be a pathological situation, and therefore must be controlled by medical practitioners, accelerated and induced. Responsibility has been transferred to 'professionals' and trust in the processes of a woman's body has been abandoned. Modern lifestyles have weakened women's bodies to the point where they find it difficult to withstand the experience and pain of childbirth.

The transfer of births from homes to hospitals destroyed the community support that women have traditionally had throughout the ages. There are no longer women surrounding the birth mother, whom she can trust to help and support her. This has led to a great deal of fear in the delivery room, which causes even greater pain during labor and eventually a loss of faith in the natural process of childbirth and in the ability inherent in a woman's body to give birth to a baby.

This 'professional' attitude is now considered 'normal' in the Western world. Like most areas in the public domain, the medical system is patriarchal, ruled by men using male instruments. The female mode of behavior -- emotional support, intuition -- is not recognized as valid or worthy of respect inside a delivery room, even though birth is strictly a womanly affair.

This reality needs to change.

The medical system's attitude toward women in labor must be able to take into account the vulnerability of the woman who arrives at the delivery room, as well as her personal history, beliefs and culture. A woman arrives with her preferences, expectations, fears and frustrations. She has her own unique body build, medical history, physical and emotional connection to her baby. She must be allowed to listen to everything that is going on inside her and to be listened to by others. Everyone must be attentive to what is going on inside of the woman.

Unless there are clear signs of medical danger, the labor should be left to happen on its own, without interference. The birth should unfold at its own time and pace without disturbing the woman's concentration.

Women during childbirth require a quiet and peaceful atmosphere, without talking or distractions, in order to focus deep within and for the hormones to be properly secreted. Women must be left in peace to be able to feel what the baby is signaling to do.

Women should be surrounded by love and trust in their ability.

Women also need to trust in themselves, in their bodies and in whoever is accompanying them. They should be free to believe in God, nature, or whatever they choose.

A birthing woman's needs should be responded to promptly and precisely. The other people in the room should support her choices and treat her and whoever accompanies her with respect. They must be aware of the fact that her body knows how to have a baby and that there are powers which guide the birth from within and without.

The birthing mother should be encouraged with kind words and compliments during her labor.

It is important that whoever is attending her be versed in matters of the heart and emotions as well as in those of the body. Expert in psychology as well as physiology. This person must be loving, wise, and know how to touch, massage and stroke the woman exactly where and when needed. To know techniques that can comfort, calm and encourage her during contractions and increase blood flow to the proper areas. If they can also sing songs to lighten the soul -- all the better.

A woman in labor needs a balance between good, useful technology and caregivers who are sensitive and have trust in her ability to have the baby. Caregivers who can consider the medical data as well as being able to see the woman in her totality of body, soul and emotions.

The birthing mother should be able to weigh the pros and cons of the situation and make use of the technology available to her without being coerced in any way. Her decisions can be based upon understanding and on choosing those options that are right for her.

She must be confident that her best interests are at heart in any decisions made about her, and not political, economic, legal or egoistic considerations.

The pregnant woman should be able to know beforehand who will be taking care of her and to choose those whom she feels will be best at empowering her and helping her to overcome her fears in the delivery room.

The medical system can and should change its relationship to women and vice versa.

We, as women, must face the reality in delivery rooms and see the hierarchy which exists in them, the ongoing power struggle between the two opposing points of view -- controlling the birth clinically or letting it happen naturally.

If the two sides can agree that our goal is the same -- a good birth for the woman and the baby -- the change will come.

The two different worldviews - one which crushes in order to control, and the other which relaxes in order to allow things to happen, exemplify the male/female dichotomy in general.

The male way is linear. -It sees a problem forms a solution and takes action. In this way of thinking the birth is a problem that must be taken care of as quickly and painlessly as possible

The female way is based on non-doing and allowing the birth to take place in its own time when the body and the baby are ready. It is not for us to control it. Birth is a healthy and joyful occurrence that the body is programmed to carry out if we will simply let it.

In order to break out of the cycle of control in delivery rooms it is necessary for women to understand that they are responsible for their own bodies and babies. To understand that pregnancy does not belong in the realm of disease, but in the realm of health.

Sayings in the delivery room such as 'a healthy child is a healthy mother' or 'we are safeguarding the health of your baby,' send a message to the birthing mother that the baby is in danger and something is likely to go wrong.

But this is not true. Birth can be risky, but it is a natural event and one of the most joyous and healthy experiences in life. When the emphasis is placed on the pathological dangers of birthing, fear and worry are heightened. The medical system allows or even wants this, because once the woman is frightened she is easy to control.

In giving birth, however, if the woman is relaxed and feels safe, the chances for an easy and successful birth are increased.

During her pregnancy, as the time of delivery draws near, a woman should take a close look at how she cares for her physical well-being and at her attitude toward pain. She should take time to learn about the physical and spiritual importance of having a baby. She should analyze the social norms which influence her and understand how the birth will unfold in ways that may lead to unnecessary intervention and to aggressive solutions.

Once she has a clear picture of reality, every woman can set a standard for herself taking into account scientific knowledge, practical know-how, her own willpower, responsibility, and ability.

By combining all these factors she can now make a conscious decision, according to her own worldview about how she would like to have her baby.

A woman who chooses an epidural creates for herself the kind of birth experience she feels is best for her. The woman who chooses to have a Cesarian section after careful consideration of all options, will feel confident and safe with that choice. The woman who wishes to undergo the natural process of labor without intervention should also be able to do so, and should be supported fully in her decision by the medical and social establishment.

I believe there should be a joining of forces between the pregnant woman and the medical staff. A mixture of the ancient wisdom which is practical and intuitive, together with the scientific knowledge available. Just being *aware* of the dilemmas involved, will help women to return to their status as life-givers and rulers of their own bodies.

In the *Gemara*, a Jewish text, it is written that the basic and primal need and right of all women in childbirth is to feel safe and protected. The *Gemara* contains a story about a blind woman in labor who asks to have a candle lit for her even though it is the Sabbath (when lighting fire is forbidden). Why is she asking for light if she is blind? Why does she insist on going against the rules about lighting fire?

But the *Gemara* states is that the woman during childbirth is exempt from following the normal laws. The wise men who wrote it go on to explain why every whim of a woman in labor must be conceded to at all times. This duty to a woman in childbirth is based on the idea that the woman must feel secure and protected for a new life to appear in the world without complications. The blind woman who asks that a candle be lit wants to know that whoever is with her will be able to see well enough to help her and this makes her calm.

So the Jewish scholars from centuries ago tell us the same thing that we heard from midwives all over the globe. A birthing woman must receive everything she asks for to reinforce her feeling of safety and the birth will go well.

I am home. I boil a small pot of water. I add allspice, a stick of cinnamon, a bay leaf, ginger, a stem of rosemary, cumin seed, cloves and a piece of avocado branch from my garden.

The water bubbles cheerfully in the pot and the warm scent wafts through the entire house.

Too bad I don't have any duck feathers or whale blubber. I add a spoonful of ghee that I made from a recipe given to me by an Ethiopian midwife whom I met not long ago.

I remember the cocoa beans I have from Peru and add them to the boiling mixture. My heart feels happy. I have put in wisdom from all the midwives, all over the world, into one little pot.

Soon I leave to attend a birth in a delivery room. I strain my potion into a bowl and bring along some excellent chocolate.

I am now ready. I have with me the love and blessing of the women of the world. I am on my way, I take up my colored bag for birthing. It contains a hot water bottle, a small massage machine, balls inside a sock to press against the back if wanted, small towels to wipe away sweat during contractions. I bring almonds, raisins and dates. I might also need energy in order to help the mother-to-be.

I have a set of homeopathic remedies in my bag as well as scented oils and herbal tinctures.

These can be used either to calm or to awaken the birthing mother. Perhaps the contractions will be too strong, or too weak.

I have remedies for any trauma that may come up, or that she arrives with. I come with all I have learned throughout the years. Breathing techniques, types of massage, physical positions for birthing (e.g. spinning babies), and I bring myself -- my love and faith and prayers and wisdom.

I step through my doorway right foot first, kiss the mezuzah, pick a few lemon geranium leaves and some flowers to brighten the room and lift our spirits.

I meet the excited couple at the entrance to the birthing center. The staff at this birthing center are attentive and accepting. The woman breathes and sways quietly as we wait to be shown to a room. There are other women in the waiting room but she concentrates only on herself. The room for natural birth is ready for us. It has soft lighting and soft comfortable furniture.

As the contractions become stronger the midwife smiles and hugs us and we are all silent. We hear only the deep breathing of the woman during her contractions. The silence creates an atmosphere of holiness in the room. I oil my hands and press her back exactly in the right place

She is completely involved within herself, and in my heart I pray for the path of the new baby.

The midwife and I exchange glances, the husband looks with love and awe at this woman who will bring their baby into the world.

The contractions are longer now, she is panting and emitting guttural sounds. She changes position and now her water breaks. The sounds she makes are different and she becomes very alert. Her eyes are closed and the sounds coming from her throat are louder; her mouth is open as she pushes.

The midwife watches but does not interfere. The woman groans loudly one more time, opens her mouth wide and gives a mighty shout as the baby emerges into the world.

The baby is placed on the new mother's chest. We are all joyful and laughing. Love fills the space. Welcome little one, welcome to your journey in this world, welcome new mother and new father.

Made in United States
Orlando, FL
05 August 2024

49992515R00137